ABOUT THE AUTHOR

DIANA MAYCHICK is entertainment columnist for the *New York Post*. She has interviewed a great many stars from Sophia Loren to Peter O'Toole, but still finds Meryl Streep the most intriguing celebrity she's ever met.

Ms Maychick graduated from Vassar College, where Meryl Streep also took her degree, and she received her Master's degree in writing from the Johns Hopkins University, where she taught creative writing. She has won Vassar's Rose Fellowship in Creative Writing and the Callenwode Prize for Writers, as well as various journalism awards.

She and her husband live in Manhattan.

MERYL STREEP
The Reluctant Superstar

Diana Maychick

NEW ENGLISH LIBRARY

For my husband – whom I met on a
Vassar rooftop.

For my mother – who sent me there to scale
intellectual heights.

Many of the photos in this book are used with grateful acknowledgment to the
New York Post.

First published in Great Britain in 1984 by
Robson Books Ltd

First NEL Paperback Edition October 1985

NEL Books are published by
New English Library,
Mill Road, Dunton Green,
Sevenoaks, Kent.
Editorial office: 47 Bedford Square, London WC1B 3DP

Printed and bound in Great Britain by
Cox & Wyman Ltd, Reading

British Library C.I.P.

Maychick, Diana
  Meryl Streep : the reluctant superstar.
  1. Moving-picture actors and actresses——United
  States——Biography
  I. Title
  791,43′028′0924   PN2287.S78

  ISBN 0–450–05869–7

CONTENTS

ACKNOWLEDGMENTS

I would never have been able to sit down and write this book had it not been for the inspiration of Meryl Streep and the kindness of strangers, and friends.

I wish to thank my editors at the *New York Post*, Roger Wood, Steve Cuozzo, Jim Mones, Jerry Tallmer, and Laurel Gross, for their help and encouragement. The entire staff of the *Post* library, especially Jack Begg and William Heller, offered considerable assistance.

At Bernardsville High School and Vassar College, Miss Streep's former teachers gladly shared their recollections.

The staff of the British Film Institute in London provided useful information about the making of *The French Lieutenant's Woman*.

Among Miss Streep's peers, I want to express my deepest gratitude to all who spoke with me, especially Dustin Hoffman, Cher, Joe Papp, Allan Carr, Norman Mailer, Keith Barish, Mary Beth Hurt, John Savage, Michael Moriarty, Jerry Schatzberg, Blanche Baker, Robert Benton, and Rose Bergunder Styron.

My agent, Ted Chichak, at the Scott Meredith agency

and my editors, Tom Dunne and Lisa Wager, at St. Martin's Press were all warmly supportive.

Most of all, I owe to my family and friends more than words can express. For their love, companionship, and conversation I wish to thank all my aunties and Margot and Vico Borgo, Debra Fine-Yohai, the Calck Hook Dance Company, Thomas King Flagg, Dr. Alan Kling, Adele Donham, Stephen Silverman, Ruth E. V. Salley, Jay Butterman, and Charles Skinner.

For professional assistance, I owe a debt to Barbara Pflughaupt, Nan Leonard, and all my fellow journalists who shared their work with me.

Finally, no work, no achievement, nothing at all, would be worth doing without Gino and Mama.

Diana Maychick
New York City

She had one of those peculiar female faces
that vary very much in their attractiveness:
in accordance with some subtle chemistry
of angle, light, mood.

John Fowles
The French Lieutenant's Woman

1

UNDOING THE IMAGE

Meryl Streep cannot escape being Meryl Streep no matter how hard she tries to be ordinary.

She steps out of a taxi in Little Italy. She walks to the driver's window to pay her fare. "Hey, aren't you a big deal?" the cabbie asks. "What are you doing down here, slumming?

"I live here," Meryl says quietly. She grabs her change, then dodges the winos and a stray ball thrown by some kids playing a street game. Dressed in a white gauze skirt and blouse, from the back she looks like a nurse, or a missionary—anyone but the most esteemed actress of her generation.

In front of her building, a converted factory on the wrong side of Manhattan's fashionable Soho, she turns for a moment.

Then it shows. It's all in her face: the sad blue eyes; a forehead so high that it seems to hold the weight of the world; wide-curved lips; and eyebrows that arch down, low down. She's upset. It's happened again. Meryl hates to be recognized.

1

Considering how much she loathes stardom, it's amazing how far Meryl has come in a profession that thrives on "the big display." In ten short years, she's traveled from the obscurity of walk-on parts in walk-up theaters to starring roles in major motion pictures. And she's done it without once allowing herself to luxuriate in acclaim.

In fact, the more successful she becomes, the more Oscars and Emmys that crowd her shelves, the more Meryl resents her fame. It intrudes on her world. When Canadian Prime Minister Pierre Trudeau once saw Meryl in a play, he was so taken with her he promptly went backstage and asked her out. She was stunned. She refused. Later, after he left, she said to an associate: "I don't understand it. Why do famous people only want to meet other famous people?"

Meryl is the most reluctant superstar ever to capture the imagination of the American public and this hesitancy may be her biggest appeal.

Her shy manner refuses to break hearts. She won't relinquish her down-to-earth ways. She's a safe idol. She's not going to die like Marilyn Monroe, nor leave her profession to marry a prince, as Grace Kelly did. She would never, you can bet on it, make a TV commercial. If you invest your dreams in Meryl, she'll pay off—but the dividend is the absence of fantasy. In screen roles such as *Silkwood* and *Kramer vs. Kramer*, she lends dignity to ordinary women. In *The French Lieutenant's Woman* and *Sophie's Choice* she takes enigmatic heroines and peels away their complexities, like the layers of an onion, until their hearts show. In all her roles, Meryl forces emotion out of simple truth. She refuses, on the screen, to upstage reality.

And in life, she certainly doesn't want reality to upstage her. This is the reason she avoids "the big display." Witness Meryl at a party. Producer Sam Spiegel, the legendary holdover from the days of highly successful movies including *On the Waterfront* and *The African Queen*, throws a bash for today's "screen legends," as he calls them. In his Park Avenue penthouse filled with Old Masters, mahogany paneling, and satin draperies, Meryl arrives and immediately lightens the mood in the room. She wears a diaphanous cotton dress that falls from her shoulders like a toga, but no jewelry and no makeup. Her face is buoyantly alive now: all cheekbones, clear as porcelain. Her eyes are shining. The woman upset by the taxi driver is not visible. It's as though she never existed.

In a corner, Meryl starts a conversation with film critic Judith Crist. It's easy to imagine they are discussing something terribly important. They retreat to the wraparound balcony that leads into Spiegel's plush living room. "Well, I've tried Pampers for the baby," Meryl says to Miss Crist, "but I just don't know. I mean, you and I we were raised on cloth diapers. What do you think? But it's hard for the delivery guy to walk up five flights; we live in a walk-up, you know, so I don't know what to do."

Her lack of pretension is occasionally disarming. At another party, she shocks guests when she talks about the lifestyle she chooses. "Well, lately," she says to a well-dressed, wide-eyed group, "I've been coming across more and more bums urinating in the halls. But I'd hate to move just because of something like that."

Is she for real?

She is so real she confounds notions of celebrity. Meryl is the first actress with whom ordinary women can truly identify.

She comparison shops, worries about her children, hates to exercise. "Exercise!" she cries. "Exercise? Oh God, no. I was athletic as a kid. And in drama school for three strenuous years I studied mime, fencing, gymnastics. After that I vowed never to get off the couch again." Then she indulges in a wicked imitation of Jane Fonda pushing her exercise tapes. "Go for the burn!" Meryl yells. "The last thing I want to do is 'go for the burn!'"

Offscreen, she may be lazy—"I depend totally on that morning call from the studio, otherwise I'd never get going. I need someone cracking the whip, or I'll spend all day reading a magazine, or listening to music, or talking on the telephone," she says—but when she's working, Meryl's going for the burn, working until she drops so that the other character, the one she's perfecting, has a chance to live.

Her one regret is that her looks sometimes get in the way. Her face is a prism of angles. "I love to photograph her," says cinematographer Nestor Almendros. "It's like photographing a Brancusi." But Truman Capote sees Meryl differently: "Her nose. That red thin sharp snout—it reminds you of an anteater. And those eyes. If they were any smaller, or closer together, you'd think she was a hen."

Meryl would like her face to elicit less controversy, if only for a wider range of roles. She jokes about the time she was making a movie with Alan Alda and during the kissing scenes, their noses "got in the way." Another time, "I went up for *King of the Gypsies*, the Dino De Laurentiis film," she says. "His son, who has since died [July 1981] in a plane crash, remarked to his father in Italian, 'But she's not beautiful.' It didn't bother me as much that he said it, as that he said it in Italian. I did Italian 105 at Vassar. I told him I understood and that it didn't matter anyway. But I never forgot it. 'What does he mean?' I told myself, 'I was voted Best Looking in my high school.'"

Other producers are so hooked by her odd beauty they forget Meryl is highly principled. She turned down glamorous parts in Sidney Sheldon's *Bloodline* and Judith Krantz's *Scruples* because, she says, "[I] won't do junk. It's my only criterion."

Yet the overriding force in her life is not work, but her family. Her husband and kids are an anchor to the world and she will allow nothing to interfere with their happiness. But the way she lives now, predicated by her success, is slightly dismaying to Meryl. "I have four kinds of insurance—life, medical, car, and property insurance—three phone lines, an accountant, two agents, a lawyer, a secretary, and a nanny," she says incredulously, counting the items off on her fingers. "My husband has an assistant; my son attends a short afternoon push-me-down called play school four afternoons a week whose tuition is $1,700 *more* than Vassar's tuition when I matriculated. We have an apartment in New York and a summer house that we use all winter, thereby heating most of Dutchess County. I have nine million bills a month. I have met more people in this short career of mine than Shakespeare and Dante met in their lives. My brothers, my friends, are all married with kids, single with kids, divorced, or living with people. I go to bed between 9:30 and 10 P.M. The network of my concerns and responsibilities has extended way, way beyond anything I could have imagined." The good old days are gone.

"When I first got to New York," she says, "I lived on West 69th Street near the park. I got three bills a month—the rent, the electric, and the phone. I had my two brothers and four or five close friends to talk to, some acquaintances, and everybody was single. I kept a diary. I read three newspapers and the *New York Review of Books*. I read books. I took afternoon naps before performances and stayed out till two and three, talking about acting with actors in actors' bars."

Meryl was learning then what she calls "the difference between the devil and the dream." She was developing a conscience and consciousness of quality. It's never left her. But in the early 1970's, when she first came to New York as a young actress, the dream was most vivid.

She arrived naive. Then the bubble burst.

2

SIX MONTHS

They were an odd couple, a couple of crazy kids in love with each other and with themselves for finding each other. It was always this way with young lovers, except these two had so many fine words in their heads that they thought their love was different.

They could love each other in Shakespeare, Euripides, Chekhov. They were Romeo and Juliet, Dante and Beatrice. They were actors.

She was regal, patrician, blonde; with a "good Dutch name," she says, "like Rockefeller." He was balding, intense, contradictory; an Italian with a cleft chin like Troy Donahue and deep black circles under his eyes.

When they read scripts together, she looked like a little girl learning her arithmetic sitting next to a monk from the Middle Ages pouring over his illuminated manuscript. His concentration burned the words right off the page and imprinted them on his brain.

Her name was Meryl Streep. His name? What was it? He died, you know. . . .

And the little girl grew up fast.

Death takes pain and spreads it thin. When John Cazale died of bone cancer on March 12, 1978, Meryl felt an ache that came from breathing itself. Her carefully constructed world fell apart. The perennial golden girl from Bernardsville, New Jersey, had to mature beyond her twenty-six years to find the inner resources to cope with her tragic loss.

They had lived together on the Upper West Side in Manhattan for two years. Cazale and Streep, the mailbox read, like a vaudeville team. Inside, it was more like a specialty shop, smoked foods perhaps, where you could find prosciutto and graavlox. But if you wanted a frankfurter, you'd be wise to go someplace else. There wasn't too much of the ordinary at Cazale and Streep's.

Oh, they shared the rent, took out the garbage, ran out of light bulbs. But the daily routine of living together mattered less to them than to other couples. They needed each other because they loved each other, not the other way around. And they had a common goal: to bring characters to life. When Cazale died Meryl not only became a widow without a marriage, she lost Romeo and Dante, too.

"I was so close that I didn't notice the deterioration," Meryl says. "John's death came as a shock because I didn't expect it."

Religion would have helped. If she could have fingered rosary beads and believed in a "divine plan," or entertained notions of reincarnation, Meryl would have had an easier time. As it was, her belief in God was tentative. Her Protestant background left her with a feeling for the Nativity crèche and the palm fronds of Easter Sunday, but she was not particularly religious. Meryl had to dig deep within herself to find a reason to continue her own life after Cazale's death. "I didn't get over it," she says. "I don't want to get over it. No matter what you do, the pain is always there in some recess of your mind."

Sadness didn't figure into the game plan of her upbringing. Meryl was reared on hearty goodwill in New Jersey's hunt country, the only daughter of pharmaceutical executive, Harry Streep II and commercial artist Mary Louise Streep. When the going got tough with outbreaks of sibling rivalry or disappointments in school, she and her brothers, Harry III and Dana, roughhoused on the rolling hills surrounding their red wooden house. They played basketball on the makeshift court near the garage. When disappointments hit, they ran and cycled and swam; they sweated away letdowns. The philosophy of Meryl's parents and their friends was that physical exertion took the mind off problems. Their suburbia was closer to the spirit of Sparta than Athens; a place where introspection was frowned upon as a sign of something alien, like a neurosis picked up from Manhattan. In this milieu, sunshine cured all ills. Nothing in Meryl's girlhood prepared her for the torture of Cazale's slow death.

School chums from Bernardsville High, Vassar and Dartmouth colleges, and Yale University remember Meryl as an outgoing girl blessed by good fortune. "Whatever she did was perfect. Everything she touched turned to gold," recalls Debbie Bozack, a friend from Meryl's high school graduating class. "It got sickening. But I guess we were all a little jealous."

Until Cazale's death, luck followed Meryl like a puppy does its master. Three days after she moved to Manhattan in 1975, she secured a part with Joseph Papp's renowned New York Shakespeare Festival. For a young actress, landing up with Papp was a coup. One year later, she met Cazale—fittingly enough, onstage in another Papp production.

These were the years when she was having the time of her life. "She was fervent about her work," says Papp. "And she was fervent about John. She took care of him as if there was nobody else on earth. She was always at his side. It was such a statement of loyalty, of commitment. She never betrayed any notion that he would not survive."

When the end was near, Meryl gave up acting to nurse Cazale day and night. Two weeks before he died, she moved into the hospital with him and "became his mother, his lover, his buddy," according to a nurse who was on duty in the cancer ward. "It was the kind of love you read about in poetry books."

When he was too weak to read, Meryl read the sports pages to Cazale. She would imitate sportscaster Warner Wolf, an overly dramatic announcer famous for yelling "swish" whenever a basketball player makes a hoop without touching the rim. Her voice became tremulous, like Wolf's, as she dramatized the exciting moments. "Let's go to the videotape," she'd say, mimicking the TV personality. "Swish!" She wanted to say it about Cazale. She wanted him to beat the odds, make the basket. She wanted him to live. And to his dying day, she thought he would.

A part of Meryl went with Cazale when he closed his eyes on that Sunday in March and died. Theirs was a young love, the kind that helps define one to oneself through the echo of another. Bit by bit, they picked up each other's habits, mannerisms, turns of phrase. Meryl's hopes and dreams reverberated in Cazale. And then there were no sounds.

Soon after Cazale died, Meryl experienced an equally profound shock. A former girlfriend of his suddenly "materialized from California and reclaimed our apartment," Meryl says. "So within three weeks, I not only lost John but our home." Meryl knew nothing about another woman, but the stranger had showed up at the apartment with the lease: a simple sheet of paper printed with tenants' rights and duties and, at the bottom, in blue ballpoint, a strange name. It bespoke a tortuous mystery. Was the relationship between Cazale and the other woman really over? Why did she hold the lease? All these thoughts passed through Meryl's head, but there was no way to untangle them. Meryl packed her bags and left, leaving behind the joy that comes from blind faith and entering a period of intense doubt.

Yet proof of the new Meryl came a short six months later, shocking her friends, maybe even herself. In a quiet ceremony in her parents' retirement home in Mystic, Connecticut, Meryl married.

His name was Donald Gummer.

Over the years her brother Harry III—a choreographer known as Third to his intimates—had introduced Gummer to his sister on several occasions. "And I never remembered him," Meryl says. He looked like any number of reformed hippies: shaggy curls, corduroy jacket, the leanness that comes from forgetting to eat. He was a thin teddy bear, the kind of guy most women want to cuddle and feed.

After Cazale died, Third took his big sister under his wing and forced her to socialize with his crowd: the New York artistic community. They were a motley crew of painters, writers, and dancers, held together by esthetics, talent, and technique. In a practical sense, their friendships boiled down to where they had gone to school. And in this clique, most of the diplomas, including the ones held by Third and Gummer, came from Ivy League schools.

Gummer is a sculptor whose big wooden and metal pieces resemble the public spectacles of one of his first teachers, David von Schlegell. "He was a star at Yale," says one artist classmate, "and he knew it. He was cocky and bright, a bit too egotistical."

While he was still in school, another teacher, sculptor Richard Serra, arranged for Gummer to exhibit his work at a two-man show at 112 Greene Street. "Not only was a student showing his work unheard of," says another artist, "but at the time, the gallery was one of Soho's best."

For about a year, Gummer basked in his progress. His pieces were receiving critical acclaim. His ideas outnumbered his output. In that first blush of success he married his high school sweetheart. Then his world began to crumble.

He experienced an excruciating period where he felt he couldn't sculpt. When a writer experiences a block, he can hide his pencil. How could Gummer avoid the huge, un-chiseled blocks of wood, the slabs of marble, the blank steel plates in his studio? It was a dreadful time of self-doubt that contributed to his divorce.

By the time Meryl met and began to remember him, Gummer was back at work. He was also living with another woman—a beautiful dancer who often shared rehearsal space with Third. After Meryl was forced to give up the apartment she had shared with Cazale, Gummer and the dancer offered to lend her their Soho loft. They were leaving for a European trip.

From this point, the plot twists and thickens in a melo-drama so sensational that if offered its script, Meryl would have turned it down.

Gummer and his girlfriend flew to Europe. Meryl moved into their apartment. Gummer returned from London early. Two months later, he and Meryl married.

It took guts to do what Meryl did next. She did nothing. She offered no feeble explanations to the dancer or their mu-tual friends about her hasty wedding.

Greta Garbo taught the world that anonymity breeds curiosity. Today the mysterious film legend has no better student than Meryl, her screen successor, an actress who also makes the headlines by studiously avoiding them. Meryl learned the lesson the hard way in 1978 when her life equaled the sensationalism of a potboiler. In March, Cazale died. By September, she was Mrs. Gummer. Into that half year, Meryl crammed a life's worth of ups and downs.

And she wished no one would take notice. From the moment she exchanged vows with Gummer, Meryl became leery of revealing too much. She wanted to return to the time before reviewers had compared her to Bette Davis, Carole Lombard, Faye Dunaway. She longed to be forgotten.

Somebody else echoed her wish. "It's still too painful for me to talk about why it's over between Gummer and me," says the dancer left behind. "If I never had to see or hear the name Meryl Streep again I'd be fine."

That scenario doesn't seem likely when it comes to Meryl Streep, the foremost actress of her generation, who's already won five Oscar nominations, two Oscars, an Emmy, and a Tony nomination. Her name is here to stay. But in Meryl's view, that's her biggest liability.

3

BEAUTY WAS THE BEAST

Mary Louise Streep, named after her mother, was a chubby kid who went through more awkward stages than a cat has lives. There's not a single shred of evidence in her early years that suggests she would become the sought-after and respected actress she is today.

In fact, the particulars of her past point toward a woman not unlike her own mother: an intelligent housewife with a side interest that helps pay the bills.

In many ways, that is how Meryl defines herself. But her side interest, a sport called acting, has catapulted her to a level of success beyond any suburbanite's dream.

Talent made the transformation possible, but the changeover is still a remarkable fluke in light of her background. Actresses rarely surface from as comfortable and ordinary an existence as Meryl's.

On June 22, 1949, in Summit, New Jersey, Mary Louise Streep gave birth to her first child, a round baby girl whose biggest booster was her father. Harry Streep II, an advertising executive with Merck Pharmaceutical, wanted to name the baby after his wife, "the woman who made it all possible." She concurred in the hospital. But after the christening, she regretted her decision. A baby was a unique person. So from the moment she addressed her child, she called her Meryl.

The Streeps were devoted, all-American parents striving for life, liberty, happiness, and a big backyard. Harry II stayed late at work and hoped for bonuses. Mary Louise freelanced as an illustrator. Their hard work and ingenuity paid off. They achieved their goals and produced two other children, a group as cherubic as the Campbell Soup kids. Soon after the birth of Meryl's two brothers, Harry III and Dana, they were able to move to Basking Ridge and then Bernardsville, wealthier nearby communities in central New Jersey. Each time they sold their house, they made a profit. Theirs was an economics lesson in how to move from middle class to upper middle class in a few easy steps. It was the American Dream made manifest.

In the beginning, Meryl didn't fit in. Until high school, she found herself "barely presentable"; her odd looks marred her childhood. She was always too big for her age. A pair of grown-up glasses formed a permanent ridge on her nose. Her left ear was bigger than her right and it stuck out. Her hair was mousy brown and frizzy. It was trimmed at home, around the kitchen table, where the normal distractions of family life always left Meryl with a short, funny fringe on her forehead. "Those are bangs, dear," her mother would say.

She was a gangly kid, all arms and legs, with a viperish tongue and a penchant for nosing into the affairs of the neighbors, the kind of child adults feared. "At seven," she says, "I looked like a forty-year-old." She acted like one, too. "The kids thought I was one of their teachers."

The neighborhood gang balked at Meryl's bossiness, but deferred to her status as the resident WASP. "With Carmine Petriccione, Pancho Solegna, and Bozo della Russo around my neighborhood, no one was making fun of my name," Meryl says.

At the turn of the century, scores of immigrant Italians settled in the Methodist enclave in the Bernardsville area and helped build the various towns with their construction skills. They remained, converted to Protestantism, and grew with the area, becoming lost in the uniformity of suburbia. By the early 1950's, the years of Meryl's childhood, the only thing different about the neighbors were their names. They were of the same bolt of cloth: everyone went to the same services on Sunday, bought their newspapers at the same candy store, put the wash out on Wednesdays, and went to the movies on Saturday night.

Meryl's father picked up all the bric-a-brac that marked 50's papadom: car seats, trampolines, Life Savers candy to placate a wailing child, and a home-movie camera to record a happy one. That Kodak camera provided Meryl's first exposure to film. She was, says her brother Harry III, "a bit of a director." In fact, she'd dress her brothers in silly costumes—her father's old fedoras, her mother's high heels—and dance them around the living room while her mother clapped and her father recorded the moment.

As to being directorial, Meryl the youngster was "a pretty ghastly" tyrant, says Harry, who first received his nickname Third from Meryl because of the Roman numeral after his name. Her position as big sister to two brothers carried over to the neighborhood, where she took control. "She was a bossy little terror," recalls one neighbor. "And pity the poor kid who didn't want to go along with whatever games she'd designated for the day." Meryl remembers herself with unflinching honesty: "I was an ugly little kid with a big mouth, an obnoxious show-off."

Even so, she got her first applause by age twelve when she sang "O Holy Night" in French in her school's Christmas concert. She was so good, in fact, that she stunned her family and classmates with the quality of her prepubescent coloratura soprano voice. Her mother says she believed Meryl's talent was "too good to waste." She made a few phone calls and found the best voice teacher in Manhattan, the internationally renowned coach Estelle Liebling. The eighty-year-old instructor was Meryl's first encounter with a true artist. She was an imposing eccentric who wore blood red lipstick and trailing scarves. In her penthouse studio at 150 Central Park South, she insisted on accompanying her students herself on an ancient Steinway baby grand that Miss Liebling called "daughter." She was a taskmaster who taught from experience, having made her debut with the Metropolitan Opera in 1903, the same year as Caruso. "He did not have a voice," she often told Meryl. "He had a trumpet."

Once a week for several years, Mrs. Streep drove her daughter to the Upper West Side and made sure Meryl studied during the hour-long ride. Her lesson was at 11:30 A.M. The hour before was taken up by a bubbly redhead, Meryl recalls, "the nice lady who had the lesson before me." Her name was Beverly Sills. "I was twelve years old and she was about to make her debut. I thought she was good. I thought I was good, too." As it turns out, however, these lessons got in the way of other activities she valued more highly. "I was," she says candidly, but with a twinge of regret, "more interested in boys and in being a cheerleader."

After four years, she quit her lessons and devoted all her time to playing out a winning performance among the boyfriends, girlfriends, and teachers in the biggest drama of her adolescent life: high school.

Cheerleading turned out to be Meryl's first role. And pragmatism helped her win the biggest part. At age fourteen she took off her corrective lenses and tossed them away. Her headstrong tendencies flourished. She refused to wear her dental braces and retainer anymore. A bottle of peroxide took care of her dull brown hair. Her family was forced to use the bathroom at odd hours since Meryl spent a long time each day glued to the medicine-chest mirror, fussing and primping. But they did so good-naturedly; this was her time to shine. "It was my make-over," Meryl recalls. "I played the blonde homecoming queen for several years." The gawky kid was gone forever.

4

RAH-RAH GIRL

To anyone who grew up in the mid-60's, Meryl's make-over would appear terribly out of place. At a time when kids were discarding standard values and rebelling against the older generations, Meryl was rebelling toward conventionality. Nearly twenty years later, she still does not question her former attitude, at a time when political conscience was the most powerful motivating force in the life-styles of the youth of America.

"Everybody's self-conscious at that age. You want to conform, be perfect, fit in, have the right shoes. You want to make sure that you're not scraggy so that everybody doesn't throw up when they look at you." Odd words from a woman who now applauds liberation and political action. But perhaps these sentiments have to do with the vacuumlike atmosphere of her years at Bernardsville High and the pressure it could put on a girl driven by her need to win popularity contests.

The ferment and torment most American teenagers experienced in the 60's was glaringly absent from Bernardsville High. "I can't remember any Vietnam protests," says

Meryl's former music teacher, Claire Callahan. "The place was very quiet. It had that bedroom mentality of New York's suburbs." It was as though the community slept through the early 60's and awakened back in 1955. "The place was removed from large concerns," says Miss Callahan. At Bernardsville High, large concerns were football, dances, movies, hairdos, and dating.

So Meryl was not alone in her conventionality. As it turns out, she was the standard by which the other students judged themselves. Recalling this period of her life, Meryl says, "I was a nice girl, pretty, athletic, and I'd read maybe seven books in four years of high school. I read *The New Yorker* and *Seventeen Magazine*, had a great vocabulary, and no understanding whatsoever of mathematics or science. I had a way of imitating people's speech that got me an A.P. [advance placement] in French without really knowing any grammar. I was not what you would call a natural scholar." Her report cards were filled with A's, with the errant C in math. But her classmates regarded her as "a girl who could do no wrong," according to Debbie Bozack, who was one of them.

It was quite a taxing performance and perhaps somewhat overwhelming. Between honors French and English Lit, the swim team, the drama club, and cheerleading practice, Meryl set her hair with tin cans to assure ramrod-straight strands, dutifully washed her face with an acne preventative called Phisohex, massaged her cuticles, and hid the beauty routines from all and sundry. She arrived at school each day "a *Seventeen Magazine* knockout," as she herself recalls with sardonic accuracy.

She was the success she wanted to be. She even had the classic high school romances with the requisite half dozen or so handsome young men vying for her favor. Her most important boyfriend, her main squeeze, was Bernardsville High football hero Bruce Thomson. He took up most of the time she allotted to the duties of dating.

Thomson, from a solid working-class family in nearby Bedminster, was the prototypically clean-cut "big man on campus." Tall and fair, he was a cutup in class who endeared himself to the students while annoying his teachers. Meryl learned a lot from him and his cronies. "My favorite part of high school was the boys who sat in the back row," she says. "They were so *funny*! So much of what I know about comedy—even the most sophisticated comedy—comes from high school, because it's such a painful, funny time. And some of the boys in the back row, who now sell real estate in New Jersey, were the most brilliantly funny people in the whole world. I was a very good audience before I ever thought of being a performer."

As for Thomson, however, his major interest actually was not cutting up. It was football. Most afternoons during the football season, he'd rush out of homeroom to don his beloved jersey and cleats. Coach Donald Ferry worked him hard on the playing field. But Thomson did his grass drills with fervor. He performed his play assignments to the letter. He pushed his body to the limits of endurance and talent. He ran, blocked, tackled, and butted helmets with resounding crashes. Meryl was there too, jumping up and down and yelling, "Thunder, thunder, thunderation." She was a cheerleader all four years, first for the junior varsity and then for the senior team.

In their yearbook, Thomson was described as "personality plus, sweet and sincere, and a fella who was always in on things." Meryl's notation read "pretty and blonde, vivacious cheerleader, where the boys are."

"She had it all together," recalls Mrs. Bozack. "But she was very nice, too. I wanted to get on the cheering squad too and every day after school, she'd take me home and we'd practice cartwheels on her lawn. When I think of my old rump now . . . but I worked hard. She was the kind of kid you wanted to please. Her mom would be in and out encouraging us. When I wasn't chosen, I think Meryl took it as a slur against her."

During football's off-seasons, Meryl sang in the chorus, worked on the school newspaper and yearbook, swam the Australian crawl on the school team, and announced the day's activities over the public address system in Principal David A. MacNicoll's office.

In freshman year, "we thought it was great if we could get a date with a senior," says Mrs. Bozack. "And we often did, but for the life of me, I can't remember their names. It was the idea of them more than anything else.

"On Saturdays, I'd pick up Meryl and Kristi Gitzendanner, maybe, oh, a whole group of us—my father had a dealership so I always had access to a car—and we'd hit Morristown Square to go shopping. Maybe Epstein's for clothes. Then we'd go back to one of our rooms, play records, do our hair, and get ready for the big night." A big night consisted of a movie, a hamburger, a ride through town, a quick tangle of arms and legs, and then home by 1 A.M.

Their weekends were filled with bonfires and dances and sporting events and theme parties. They organized a "baby party" where members of the class dressed in diapers. They had a sophomore "sweater dance." For their junior prom, they decorated the gym with castle turrets and moats in keeping with the theme, "In the Days of Yore."

When Thomson started asking Meryl for dates, "she liked the idea of him," said one classmate. "It wasn't the romance of the century, for her. It was a way to pass the time. They looked good together, that was what I think she liked. But Bruce thought it would last forever. That happened a lot at Bernardsville High. A lot of them graduated, got married, the whole bit."

Meryl and Thomson were "nice kids," says guidance

counselor and science teacher Ronald Bernard. "Oh, they weren't goody-goodies. I recall I once saw them smooching near the side of the school, where the bushes are. She was a real cutie-pie."

But there were other boys in Meryl's life and she had quite a reputation for breaking hearts. Michael Booth, another football star from the class of '66, "was madly in love with her," recalls another classmate. "He never got over it. Last I heard, he went to South America. He always thought he'd get Meryl in the end."

Besides being chased by boys, her many activities included acting, of course, or, rather, competing for the lead in the school musicals and plays. It was only after her first taste of theater that she thought of high school as a mere stepping stone to bigger things. After all, something special was bound to happen. Meryl was never a dreamer. On the contrary, she was a highly pragmatic kid for whom a good time would never be enough. She got through high school by living in the future tense.

In the Streep household, the three children were allotted special days, in addition to their birthdays, to do whatever they chose. Meryl's favorite day was when she picked a Broadway matinee for her treat: *The Music Man*. From the opening number she fell in love with singer Barbara Cook as the part of Marian the librarian. Meryl cried at "Goodnight, My Someone" and yearned for the man Miss Cook sang about in "My White Knight." To a young girl like Meryl, this promise of future happiness was something to treasure. She saw herself in the proper, evasive, but knowing Marian. The play was corny, but the seventy-six trombones won Meryl's heart. In the tenth grade, when the school's annual musical production turned out to be *The Music Man*, she auditioned for the part of Marian the librarian.

"If I could locate the moment I was first bitten, that was it," says Meryl.

It was the most rudimentary of theater experiences. Rehearsals were called "play practice" and they took place in stolen moments when nobody was singing in choir, practicing a cheer, or redoing a science lab. The stage was small. The costumes consisted of makeshift contributions by the PTA. But Meryl remembers, "The whole audience stood up when I came out. Mind you, I've never had that experience since. It must have been like what Lady Diana felt on the balcony after her wedding to the Prince." Meryl couldn't wait to get out of high school and onto a bigger stage.

She amazed her teachers. Jean Galbraith, who taught English, remembers dropping in on a rehearsal while Meryl was singing "Till There Was You." "I thought, that can't be the kid in the first row who sits near the windows? I mean, that's professional, that's fantastic."

Jealousies surfaced among the other student actors who felt Meryl was getting far too much attention. "A lot of them felt that Meryl shouldn't be given the starring roles in all the productions," recalls Mrs. Edna Bolash, the school secretary, whose son Vincent was in Meryl's class. "We had this other girl who was quite talented too, but she really didn't get a crack at any of the big parts with Meryl around." During the play's run, Meryl didn't get any phone calls at home asking her to join the gang.

Third, who played Winthrop in *The Music Man*, said things got worse when she landed the leads in *Li'l Abner* and *Oklahoma!* But the drama department felt it had no choice but to cast Meryl. "When she walked onto the stage, there was nobody else there," says another teacher, Dick Everhart.

Her high school friends and associates assumed she would become a musical actress. But Meryl said she had no interest in pursuing that kind of acting. "All I'd seen were the big musicals with Mary Martin or Ethel Merman. I just didn't think I had the kind of energy to do that." Nor did she have the inclination to further alienate her friends. She began

23

to consider serious drama as a hobby. In that corner of acting, at least no one could accuse her of choosing the stage for
its razzle-dazzle rewards. Or so she thought. She knew nothing about the dramatic stage. She admits, "I never saw a real
play, a serious one, until I was in one."

But her last year of high school postponed any serious
considerations about her future. She had other things on her
mind. In her senior year, she was crowned homecoming
queen at the prom. For a girl who groomed herself for the
part, it was a rude awakening. There was nothing else she
could achieve. She wondered if indeed there was life after
high school.

For many of her classmates the halcyon days did end
with graduation, as Meryl discovered later at the tenth-anni-
versary high school reunion.

Meryl was one of the first to arrive. The festivities at the
Ryland Inn on Route 22 in Whitehouse, New Jersey, com-
prised a time-warp of her youth: big striped tents and picnic
tables filled with hamburgers, hot dogs, Italian sausages, and
cold salads. Two big cakes welcomed back the 100 or so
classmates from Bernardsville High '66 and '67, and their
spouses. The two open bars were well attended. Meryl and
Gummer were treated like royalty by her adoring classmates.
The brisk October 3 afternoon reminded Meryl of football
weather as the stern gusts of wind ripped through the reunion crowd. She searched the faces for an old boyfriend.
He didn't attend. Ten years later, he was balding and
paunchy from the effects of not much success and too much
beer. "He gained a lot of weight after school," recalls one of
his classmates. "He didn't do much. He was afraid to see
Meryl. The gulf between them was already too wide." Once
again, Meryl's success got in the way.

5

PINK & GRAY

Vassar College changed Meryl's life. But it was a fortuitous twist of fate that landed her at the prestigious women's college. Had it not been for an unsuccessful interview at another liberal arts college, she would not have enrolled there. During the summer after her junior year at Bernardsville High, Meryl had her heart set on Bennington College in Vermont. "I always liked New England," Meryl recalls, "and I heard good things about Bennington." Her father drove her there for the initial look-see.

And it turned her off.

"This woman interviewed me," Meryl recalls. "She said, 'Ahhh, what books have you read over the summer?'

"I looked at her. I said, 'What do you mean, books over the summer?!' I had read none. I was on the swim team.

"'Do you mean,' she said, 'that you haven't read any books over the summer?'

"I thought, oh yeah, I did go down to the library one day because it was raining and picked up this book and read it cover to cover. It was called *Dreams*.

"I thought it was fascinating, so I told her all about it.

She asked who had written it. I said, 'Carl Jung.' *J* like in jugular. She said, 'Please, Jung.' *J* like in young. I said, 'Daddy, take me home.' I mean, that was the biggest book that anyone ever read over any summer, and she's yelling at me because I don't say the name right!"

At Vassar College, her second choice—a position with which the college would hardly feel comfortable—Meryl had a lot of intellectual catching-up to do. A kid who had read only seven books in high school was now face-to-face with class valedictorians and full-time intellectuals, girls whose idea of Saturday night was an extra chunk of free time to conduct a biology experiment. "On entering," she says, "if you had asked me what feminism was I would've thought it had something to do with having nice nails and clean hair." She arrived "interested in boys, when everybody here was female. I think that fact was the single most important catalyst for change in my life to that point. Change in thinking, change and growth of mind and imagination."

It was not so much the idyllic campus on the outskirts of Poughkeepsie, dotted with lakes and farms and architectural treasures, that opened Meryl's eyes to a larger world. Nor was it necessarily Vassar's rigorous academic program. It was not even its roster of illustrious alumnae, including Edna St. Vincent Millay and Mary McCarthy, or its even more famous dropouts, Jane Fonda and Jacqueline Bouvier Kennedy Onassis.

The transformation took place, she says, because for her first two years there, Vassar still excluded men. "When I got to Vassar, my life changed because I met the most wonderful women." From head librarian Barbara LaMont to English professor Jeane Geehr, from the dorm housemothers, called White Angels, to the cleaning staff, known as Green Ladies, Meryl lived in a community of active, supportive women where the students were the mere frosting on the cake. And it was not unusual for these students to spend every waking hour together. But this was no hen party. The days were passed in exploring hopes and dreams, and in dissecting faults. In this atmosphere Meryl swallowed ideas, hungered after thoughts, and lived the mind/body duality she was learning about in philosophy class. After having paid an inordinate amount of attention to the physical in high school, her newly unrestrained mind devoured academia in a great feast of intellectuality. Meryl was escaping the hollowness of her childhood.

Surrounded by brainy women who spent their evenings in cubbyholes at the library, who daily took sherry at 4 P.M. in beat-up old clothes and heatedly discussed Kierkegaard, who associated curlers with the ice game played with brooms and not, as they would have said, with "instruments of torture" for the hair, Meryl absorbed the lessons that came from another world. So that she would never lose touch with the new realities she was seeking to understand, she would cart her books everywhere—on bus trips to the local five-and-dime, to the dining room in her dorm, to Sunday chapel. Under sprawling sycamore trees and umbrellalike lindens, she would read the Brontës, Sir Thomas Malory, and Jean-Paul Sartre. When friends came to visit Meryl and her suite mate, Jane Bradley, they had to force Meryl to relax. They would bring beer, borrow glasses from the dorm kitchen, and make her take a break. And Meryl adored it all.

"I felt absolutely great in that atmosphere," she says. "And I blossomed. Suddenly, I felt accepted by the entire other half of the human race. From the time I entered college until now, I never felt the need to compete with anyone. That just all went out the window. At Vassar, it was commonplace to give your best shot, so that became a habit. I learned to believe in myself. I acquired a genuine sense of identity."

She began to regret her "petty concerns" in high school. As she puts it, "In high school there was generally one acceptable way to be, and it was dictated by the exigencies of dating. There are those people who try to be that way, and there are the other, clunky, disastrously uncool individuals, the nerds, who swim upstream in those waters.

"I had come from this socially cutthroat, huge, coeducational high school, where if you wore the wrong shoes or showed up with the wrong guy at the dance, you were finished.

"Vassar was full of nerds, the idiosyncratic strange ones, the smart weird ones, the undatables. It had its share of high school big shots, too, like me, but we all sank or swam together."

But each weekend knifed female camaraderie in the back. Every Friday at 3 P.M., the dorms on the quadrangle emptied. Buses in front of the main gate stood ready to take hundreds of women to Yale, Vassar's brother school in New Haven, site of the mixer, a dance social commonly known at Vassar as "the meat rack." Looks counted again, but "at least the spawning grounds," as Meryl calls them, were physically distant from the seat of learning, "the sexual competition far removed."

She went to the mixers with her roommates, and taught a few of them to dance and how to make small talk with hulking preppies in striped ties. They occasionally stayed over until Sunday night if the guys were cute. "But it was a game," one graduate recalls. "We slept with them primarily because it gave us something to talk about during study breaks."

In her freshman year, Meryl lived on Vassar's quadrangle, a less desirable spot than secluded Cushing House or Main Building, an imposing maroon edifice modeled on Versailles. She and her roommates listened to Meryl's Johnny-Mathis records—"the largest collection in the world," according to one of them—and occasionally ventured out to Pizzatown, an unusual bar on Collegeview Avenue where owner George says he delighted in mixing huge drinks to "loosen up the snooty women." She traveled around the country with the school choral group, the Night Owls. She helped coordinate Sophomore Parents Weekend, where her father proudly danced with her. Unlike high school, in college she sandwiched in her activities between studying.

"It was a great time," she says. "I remember feeling: I can have a thought. I can say 'asshole.' I can do anything, because everything is allowed. Oh, it was a great relief."

In Introduction to Drama, she got up one day and "did" Blanche DuBois, the frustrated Southern belle in Tennessee Williams's *A Streetcar Named Desire*. Sitting in the middle of Avery Hall, the former horse stable that housed the English and drama departments, her teacher and director, Clint Atkinson, thought he was dreaming. So many of the Vassar women were pretentious actresses, without a clue to the characters they essayed. But this Meryl Streep was something else. "You're good," he yelled from the back of the auditorium. "You're good! Read *Miss Julie*."

The August Strindberg play, a bitter indictment of women, perplexed Meryl, but she came to appreciate the aristocratic, decadent title character after several readings. "One of our directors, Clint Atkinson, asked me, 'Why don't we do *Miss Julie*," recalls Evert Sprinchorn, then head of Vassar's drama department. "I said no. I didn't want to see it butchered, and it has only three roles. So Atkinson said, 'Well, why don't you come to a reading tonight and see what you think.' So I went and after about ten minutes, I saw that Meryl was just outstanding. It hit you right in the eye. I looked at Atkinson across the table and nodded yes."

So it happened that the first serious drama Meryl ever encountered was the one she starred in at Vassar. "I didn't care what it was about!" Meryl says. "All I knew was that I got to take this ax and cut off the head of a canary, and my

29

friends in the second row would be screaming, Oooooh! Arghhyuchhhhhh! I loved it!"

Some students felt she was overacting, but the majority of Vassar women were impressed. Her triumph spread from dorm to dorm until it was impossible to secure a pair of tickets to *Miss Julie*.

Atkinson helped Meryl's unofficial public relations campaign when he called her "a brilliant actress. There was a volcano within her. I found her acting hair-raising, almost mind-boggling," he says, adding that she played Miss Julie "with a voluptuousness that was almost shocking in someone that age. Onstage something happened within her that glowed. Men were always falling in love with her."

Among their number was John Childs, who was a Princeton student visiting for the weekend Meryl performed. "She was all the girls wanted to talk about. I came, frankly, to pick somebody up. Vassar was near the top of the list for available women, just after Sarah Lawrence, but way ahead of Mount Holyoke. That weekend, though, all they wanted to do was discuss that play. I hadn't even seen it, but I heard so much about Meryl, I fell for her description. There was a heated argument about whether or not she was involved with the director, but one girl said that was impossible. So I looked her up on Sunday, but I guess she was rehearsing."

Meryl worked in all phases of theater—directing, stage managing, lighting, and sound. She sold tickets, ushered, and functioned as a producer when she wanted to do a Molière play. She designed costumes for the student production of Tennessee Williams' *Camino Real*. And she began to fall in love with the profession, although at the time she still thought "it was no way to make a living."

By her sophomore year, any traces of the rah-rah girl were gone for good. She dressed in her father's old button-down shirts, a crumpled felt hat, and jeans. Even when she donned the school colors, pink and gray, she was only wearing an old Vassar sweat shirt. In fact, it was a new role. During Christmas vacation, when old friends commented on her appearance, she was curt. "I don't need to impress anyone." Their plaid skirts and circle pins were relics of her youth. Although she did continue to bleach her hair, in college Meryl was, by her own definition, "a slob. Let's just say my standards of personal hygiene slipped a bit." One can also say that, since this new dress code fit in very neatly with the style of even the most self-conscious of artistic Vassar students, Meryl was once again wholly involved in her immediate surroundings.

During her junior year, the first men arrived at Vassar and the school had to adjust. The college was grudging in its welcome. The women felt tricked. Had they not accepted men, Yale was willing to swallow up Vassar's female student body. A plan was broached whereby the Poughkeepsie campus would be abolished in favor of a coed Yale. Men were thus a last resort for Vassar, their admittance a tactic of self-preservation.

When they moved in, the demitasse and sherry parties disappeared. The dorms went coed and it wasn't unusual to find men and women showering in adjoining stalls—and occasionally in the same ones. Meryl had to adjust, too.

"Some of the subtler eccentricities went underground," she says about the invasion of men. "I remember my first coed year when suddenly it seemed that the editorships of the literary magazine, the newspaper, the class presidency, and the leadership of the then very important student political movements were all held by men."

She learned about feminism firsthand and refused to join the antiwar protests because she had no respect for its leaders. "It was the first year Vassar was coed," she recalls, "with 40-some men and 1,600 women. But the whole strike committee was boys; they took over and got off on it. I'm so sensitive to theater, and these boys would get up and perform. Everybody was a miniature Abbie Hoffman in front of a swarm of adoring girls. I just thought it was bullshit."

The school was in a state of flux and so was Meryl. It didn't take long for Vassar "to evolve," she says, "but personally I was grateful for my first two years, for the two-year hiatus from the sexual rat race."

During college, she developed her first close relationships. "I made female friends," she says, "ones whom I actually trusted." It was a revelation. On a small scale, in her insular little world, she also began to feel the pressures of stardom. Some students thought "she was a cold actress, an overacting brownnose."

The situation was similar to lines spoken by Miss Julie in Strindberg's play:

> That reminds me of a dream I sometimes have in which I'm on top of a pillar and can't see any way of getting down. When I look down, I'm dizzy; I have to get down, but I haven't the courage to jump. I can't stay there and I long to fall but I don't fall. There's no respite.

They were Meryl's sentiments, too. Throughout her career, she'd been on alert for the fall. And sometimes, she longed for it. When you're paid to fool people, once in a while you want to get caught, if only to prove there's a person behind the acting mask.

As a Vassar honors student, Meryl was allowed to participate in an exchange program with other Seven Sister or Ivy League schools. Meryl felt a year away would dissipate the students' jealousies. During her senior year, she chose to attend Dartmouth, in Hanover, New Hampshire, where the ratio of men to women was 100 to 1. "That's a true statistic," Meryl says, with a shake of the head and a deep laugh. It was the opposite of life at Vassar. "I experimented with being the outsider in coeducation."

But the experience wasn't a pleasant one. Dartmouth men were as unaccepting of invasions by the opposite sex as Vassar women had been. They considered females an aberration on their turf. In classes, they dominated discussions; after classes, they wanted pretty girls on their arms. The last thing they wanted from a woman was a serious discussion.

"I was lonely," Meryl says about Dartmouth. "I didn't want dates." At Vassar, she realized, "I had friends, boys and girls. At Dartmouth the men just weren't used to women walking around the campus. It upset them. We were either sex objects or ignored. They just didn't know how to deal with us as people. It was a very strange feeling."

So she threw herself into her studies: courses in costume design, dance, and playwrighting. She wrote "funny feminist dramas" and tried to round up a few willing souls to stage readings. It didn't work. The community was splintered by off-campus living arrangements, and Meryl suffered from a long commute, too. After spending an hour or two in the library, she'd rush home every day to an old house on the Connecticut River that she shared with other students. "We'd go out to the front yard to catch some striped bass and have it for breakfast. That is one of my fondest Dartmouth memories. You can't imagine the taste of this fish right off the hook!"

The grading system at Dartmouth both upset and pleased her. There she got straight A's. "My eyes crossed when I got the printout. At Vassar they had a party in the English department when the first A was given out in twenty years. At Dartmouth, it seemed to me, A's were conferred with ease and detachment. Ah, I said to myself, that's the difference between men's and women's colleges." Her voice takes on the sonorous timber of John Houseman doing a

Smith Barney commercial. At Vassar, she says, "we made A's the old-fashioned way. We earned them."

She missed Vassar so much she cut short her stay at Dartmouth and returned to Poughkeepsie for the second half of her senior year. During spring break, Clint Atkinson invited Meryl to make her New York City debut in Tirso de Molina's *The Playboy of Seville*. He directed the off-off-Broadway production at Cubiculo Theater on West 51st Street. The cast included several Equity members; one was Michael Moriarty, the production's original Don Juan, who impressed the other, mostly student actors from New York University. "It was a cliquish group," says Kieran Crowley, a writer who acted in the 1971 production. "Not much socializing." Few in the cast remember Meryl. "I was one of the easiest conquests of the Playboy," Meryl recalls. "In the play, that is."

After the three-weekend run in April, Meryl returned to Vassar to finish her papers, pack her bags, and get out. As soon as civil rights activist Eleanor Holmes Norton delivered the commencement address to the class of 1971, Meryl picked up her diploma and headed for a small theater group in Vermont.

6

GETTING EVEN

The Green Mountain Guild was not an auspicious starting point for Meryl's first stab at professional acting. The loosely knit group of young thespians survived hand-to-mouth by bringing Shakespeare and Chekhov to colleges and ski resorts. After watching their sons and daughters change costumes in small kitchens only to be booed by ski bums, a lot of parents, dismayed by what they perceived as a waste of their kids' college educations, forced their children to come home. Not Meryl's family. They followed her from resort to resort, cheering her on.

"I made forty-eight dollars a week and it wasn't even the Depression," she remembers. "But we lived in this beautiful old house—one that I surely couldn't afford now—donated to us by the wonderful old lady who liked to support the arts."

Performing, however, left much to be desired. "I could hear the people snoring in the bars and the snowmobiles outside," Meryl says. "When the lights went out, the show went on with candlelight."

But her romance with life on the road, with traveling to

small ski burgs where people couldn't care less about theater, soon faded. "I figured if I wanted to act, there was more than this," she says. "In each little role I did in front of the ski audience, I gave more of my attention to it, and I had always been kind of scattered, so that was an event. I knew it was not enough to be an actress in the snows of Vermont. I knew that if I was deciding to do this something, I ought to do it right."

It had begun. Her drive towards perfection was finally centered on something tangible. She now knew she wanted to act. But she was without any money to get started. She had little choice but to move back to Bernardsville, where she secured a waitressing job at a local beanery and began saving for graduate school tuition. While serving burgers and fries, she reviewed her options.

When it was time to make up her mind regarding drama school, the decision was easy. "The entrance fee at Juilliard was fifty dollars," she recalls. "More than I was making a week." Yale's fee was only fifteen dollars, so she applied, auditioning in the roles of two legendary women: Tennessee Williams's Blanche DuBois and Shakespeare's Portia. "I didn't know what I was doing, but they let me in anyway."

Money was tighter than ever before in the Streep household. Both brothers were in college. Her father was considering retirement. Meryl survived financially with the help of a scholarship; in addition, she waited on tables and typed papers for spending money.

"Once I got in, there was no going back," she says. Yale recognized her talent and worked her to the bone; she played in forty productions during her three years there. She also fought with her teachers, developed an ulcer, and visited a psychiatrist.

She played Helena in *A Midsummer Night's Dream*; Bertha, the high-strung daughter in Strindberg's *The Father*;

Hallelujah Lil in *The Happy End*, by Bertolt Brecht and Kurt Weill. With each new role the tension grew.

"Every year, there'd be a coup d'etat. The new guy would come in and say, 'Whatever you learned last year, don't worry about it. This is going to be a new approach.'" So she closed her eyes, tried to forget the previous technique, and went through all sorts of crazy exercises, including one where she delivered numbers instead of words. "We did a version of [Chekhov's] *The Three Sisters* that way," she says. "I was Masha. One of my lines was: Three, five, five, five, seven, two, eight." Then she learned about "emotional recall" from a teacher who, she recalls, "delved into our personal lives in a way I found obnoxious." The sense of competition grew. Some students buckled under and dropped out.

Graduate work "was terribly intense," Meryl remembers. "That kind of grab-bag, eclectic education is invaluable, but only out of adversity. Half the time you're thinking I wouldn't do it that way, this guy is full of crap, but in a way, that's how you build up what you do believe in. Still, those years made me tired, crazy, nervous. I was always throwing up." But she was as headstrong as ever, according to fellow student Christopher Durang, now a playwright.

"In an acting project, she was cast as the queen and I as her son in Brecht's *Edward the Second*," he recalls. "We rehearsed it for a couple of weeks and it wasn't going well. Now, the director had mentioned that he wanted to use a circus conceit in the staging, but when the costume parade came around, Meryl was dressed like a trapeze artist: she had beads on her chest, beads on her crotch—they made noise whenever she walked. Well, Meryl put this on and shot the director a look of daggers. She said there was no way she'd perform in that outfit." She did do it—but without the beads.

During her first year, her acting teacher Thomas Haas

shocked Meryl by placing her on academic warning. "He said that I was holding back my talent out of fear of competing with my fellow students. There was some truth in that, but there was no reason to put me on warning. I was just trying to be a nice guy, get my M.A., and get out of drama school."

Durang and playwright Albert Innaurato, another member of Meryl's class, recollect with glee the time she got even with Haas. It was during a performance of their joint effort, a musical comedy called *The Idiots Karamazov*. Meryl was playing the lead: an ancient, crippled, mad Russian translator, Constance Garnett at the end of her life.

"Tom Haas directed the student production," says Durang of his farce, "and he had it in for Meryl. He also thought Meryl took too much focus away from another character's speech at the end; Haas told her to do less. So she did. But when the curtain calls came, Meryl improvised by rolling herself around the stage in her wheelchair, screaming, 'Go home! Go home!' Then she faked a heart attack. It was hilarious. And she got even."

Innaurato was more impressed by her acting technique. "She invented the part," he says, "marvelously transforming herself into that eighty-year-old *littérateuse*. She even sang a Barbra Streisand parody—and it was not a betrayal of the work. She pulled it off. She's a genius."

"I adored playing Constance," Meryl says. "Anyone in a wheelchair! It's bound to be great. It limits you and at the same time it frees you." Robert Lewis, another of her Yale drama professors and one of the founders of the famed Actors Studio, says her Constance was "the most imaginative farcical performance I've ever seen."

He also has high praise for her portrayal of Alma in Tennessee Williams's *Summer and Smoke*. "It was certainly the best I ever saw that part played, and that's a reaction you don't usually feel when students do scenes, you know. It was so clinical you could hardly look at it. It was like looking into somebody's life."

Meryl's three years at Yale were all work and no play. Even her good friend, classmate Joe Grifasi, recalls few times when she wasn't working. He got to know her while they walked from the dorms to the theater and the classrooms. He remembers one incident when her talent for improvisation shone through.

When an actor missed a cue, Meryl was left alone onstage for several long minutes. "The setting was a psychiatrist's office," Grifasi says, "and Meryl walked around, picking up objects and finally peering intently at the Rorschach inkblot pictures on the wall. Then she looked at the audience as if she had discovered a major flaw in her character and burst into tears."

The real defect Meryl discovered in herself. The pressure of "crawling inside twelve to fifteen people each year" had gotten to her.

"I would go in and say, 'I can't do any more.' And of course they would say to me, 'Pressure? What pressure? You think this is bad, wait till you get out of here, will you have problems!'"

Her psychiatrist told her she wouldn't have any problems as soon as she got out of Yale. "And you know what," says Meryl, with a certain amount of satisfaction, "the minute I got out, I didn't have any more problems."

She spent her summer at the Eugene O'Neill Playwrights' Conference, an annual tryout of new plays in Connecticut. Producers came to look over the material with an eye toward the select few worth producing. What they discovered that year was not a play. What they found was Meryl.

7

A SMALL CIRCLE OF FRIENDS

Meryl had a degree in her right pocket, another one in her left, an ulcer in her stomach, and no job. What kind of job was she prepared for anyway, after seven years squirreled away in the hinterlands of Poughkeepsie, Hanover, and New Haven? After the SAT's and GMAT's that placed her in schools and left her armed with an A.B. from Vassar and an M.F.A. from Yale, Meryl would have to pass another test to act in the real world. "I thought: I'm twenty-six, I'd better make it soon."

Pencil and paper didn't work for this test, but it still had its own set of initials: TCG, as in Theater Communications Group. And of all the letters of the alphabet, these three were the most important to a young person who wanted to be on a stage other than a college proscenium.

At a mass audition more crowded and frightening than a Moonie group wedding, the chaff of acting humanity was separated from the wheat. Meryl looked like the wheat: slender, tall, and blonde, a flaxen stem. In this summer of 1975, she appeared to be quality goods. A perfect Ophelia, perhaps, or the younger sister of a lead? The stages offered by TCG were small, serious, regional ones in places like Chicago, Minneapolis, Baltimore.

Yale had prepared her well. It even offered a popular course on how to audition for TCG. "It was unbelievable," Meryl says. "Everybody had their two pieces ready—the serious one [her voice drops a register]—and the comic one [a high tweet]."

The two pieces were always "the Shakespeare and the modern," she says. On the night before the audition, Meryl came to New York, stayed with friends, and went to sleep early.

"The next morning I woke up, looked at the clock, and went back to sleep." It was the biggest chance she had and she slept through it. "I simply didn't go."

At the time, she felt scared and a little irresponsible. "I thought: now you've done it. It's all over. You're finished." Later, she could picture the scene in the hotel banquet hall where the auditions took place. There are a group of actors, many of them her classmates, awaiting her late arrival. Her mouth is open, eyes wide. She begins to mimic her peers: "Ooooh, for gawd's sakes, where's Meryl?! Ooooh, for gawd's sakes, she's really fucked herself now. . . . Oh, man, you know . . . is she fucked!"

Instinctively, she must have felt that she was too good to spend the next five years working at a small regional company, working her way back to New York. She decided to take a chance.

There are informal, but still dutifully honored, rules and regulations in the theater world. One does not, for instance, arrive at a theater and beg a casting director for an audition. But that's exactly what Meryl did.

She went to Rosemarie Tichler at Joseph Papp's Public Theater. Casting queen Tichler has a second-floor office filled with theater memorabilia: posters of hit shows, *Playbills*, scripts. She has a big old desk, a deep brown rug, lots of wicker furniture, and seashells under glass. It's a comfy place, more like a Victorian lady's dressing room than a casting office. But Meryl wasn't comfortable. There was one dead giveaway to Miss Tichler's power. In the midst of all the pretty little things sits the hugest, and some say most valuable, Rolodex in New York. With it, Miss Tichler can wake Al Pacino and ask him if he wants a part. She can ring Estelle Parsons at her mother-in-law's place. She has the numbers of shrinks specializing in actor's neuroses—just in case. On her first visit, Meryl stared at the revolving wheel of phone listings.

"I begged her to give me an audition," Meryl says. "She asked why I wasn't at the TCG audition. I told her I was having stomach trouble. She said, 'Well, all right.' And she saw me. And she said, 'I may have something for you.' And that's how," she said with a note of irony and triumph and disbelief, "I got the part of the manager in *Trelawny of the Wells*."

Theater insiders, especially that small band of marginal directors, actors, and wardrobe mistresses who thrive on promoting myths about their profession, were breathless at Meryl's immediate success. Then they quickly turned wry. "Ah, so you were in *Trelawny of the Wells*," says one director to an actor auditioning for him. "Then you must have been there when Meryl Streep first appeared on the New York stage and the world came to a halt."

Aptly enough for her first professional appearance in New York, Meryl played an actress, manager of a small theatrical stock company called the Wells, in the revival of Arthur Wing Pinero's 1898 comedy. And her costars became friends for life. Most of them would continue their careers, but Meryl would later outshine each one.

Mary Beth Hurt played the leading role of Rose Trelawny, a fading ingenue actress who considers giving up the stage for a man with money in his pockets. Mandy Patinkin, whom Meryl nearly worked with on *Ragtime*, played Rose's boyfriend. John Lithgow played an old-fashioned actor in the troupe. Although her part was small, Walter Kerr singled out Meryl in his generally negative review of the production. "In the overstressed onrush," he wrote in *The New York Times*, "only two figures emerge at all: Meryl Streep as a glossily successful former colleague who has gone on to 'star' in another theater, tart, level-headed, stunningly decked out in salmon gown and white plumes; and Mary Beth Hurt, as Rose Trelawny herself."

From that point on, the Public Theater became Meryl's second home. "It's the only place in New York where you can walk in totally unknown and get a hearing," she raves to young actors. "And then a chance to appear in a major production."

Two days after Meryl landed her part at the Public, the Phoenix Theater called. Would she be interested in auditioning for two one-act American plays for their bicentennial celebration? Of course. Once the interest in Meryl began, it never stopped.

Throughout its illustrious thirty-year history, the Phoenix Theater, under the directorship of T. Edward Hambleton, encouraged new playwrights and actors to work together without fear of losing money. And in 1976, the theater was no different. Meryl auditioned for Tennessee Williams's *27 Wagons Full of Cotton* and Arthur Miller's *A Memory of Two Mondays*. She got both parts.

"It all seemed too easy," Meryl says about landing both parts. Easy and, frankly, unbelievable.

Flora in *27 Wagons Full of Cotton* is a 170-pound, poor white trash Southerner who is terrorized and later seduced by her husband's business competitor. She verges on being an imbecile. She is downright pathetic. She was not the kind of woman immediately recognizable to theater audiences. Although the play was written in the 1940's, it wasn't produced until 1955, when Maureen Stapleton initiated the role. The only thing Miss Stapleton and Meryl have in common besides their acting talent is each one's ability to laugh at herself. It came in handy during Meryl's audition.

She arrived, her slim self, wearing blue jeans and a T-shirt. Before her turn to read, Meryl hurried to the ladies' room and stuffed a supply closet's worth of paper towels down her pants and shirt. "I'd guess that when I came out of the ladies' room I was a 40 D," she says. "But I wasn't fooling anyone. It was mostly for myself, to get the feeling of bulk I needed to feel like Flora."

The casting agents were aghast at her juvenile tactics, but once they heard her read, they quickly changed their minds. Her accent was "outrageously overdone," she recalls. But nobody quite heard or saw the ordinary truth. "Meryl gave the pathos a certain lyrical dignity," says Hambleton. Director Arvin Brown hired her immediately.

Onstage with Ray Poole as her husband and Tony Musante as the superintendent of another farm, Meryl was sexy, dim-witted, raunchy, comical, and earthily wise. She gave the character a past and future just in the way she spoke her lines. Here was a real woman, Meryl seemed to say; she's more than meets the eye.

"It was really great fun," she says about Flora. "I got a big cleavage with one of those prosthesis bras—it was the first time I had ever even seen a D cup—and I wore a body suit built with a tummy and a butt."

Big Flora Meighan gave her something else she'd wanted: the opportunity to prove that a homecoming queen from New Jersey can play more than ingenues. "That role did a lot to help me crash through that barrier," she says.

The Miller play, which also featured her new friend John Lithgow as a long-suffering poet, was performed immediately after *27 Wagons Full of Cotton*. During the short intermission, Meryl had to become a totally different character: a trim, brunette secretary named Patricia who works in an auto parts factory during the Depression.

As soon as the curtain rose for the second half of the evening, playgoers began to squirm in their seats. They'd rustle their programs, find Meryl Streep's name twice, and whisper uncomfortably.

"What the people said fed into what I wanted for myself, which was not to be typecast," Meryl says. Still, the audience was stunned to realize they were seeing the same actress. "That sort of thing is done all the time," Meryl says knowingly, "but to do it on the same night was considered pretty impressive."

27 Wagons Full of Cotton was so well-received that Meryl got a Tony nomination, in addition to a Theater World and Outer Critics Circle Award. This sort of acclaim was unheard of for an actress with so little professional stage experience. After it, she never had to go to another open audition, do TV commercials, or wait on tables, the usual occupations of a beginning performer. She leapt into the big time. And while her story became a source of jealousy to some young actors, others dreamt about it nightly. It's the kind of overblown, unbelievable good fortune that daily feeds the aspirations of the acting profession.

When Mary Beth Hurt and John Lithgow began talking about a new Phoenix production, *Secret Service*, Meryl decided to take a look and see if there was a part that might challenge her. She found one. And Joe Grifasi, her Yale buddy, also came aboard.

The revival of *Secret Service*, a Civil War spy thriller written in the late nineteenth century by William Gillette, was done in a tongue-in-cheek fashion that irked some critics. Meryl played the heroine, a lovesick belle enraptured by a Lithgow, who played a muddled, twitching captain in the Confederate army who turns out to be a Union spy. Miss Hurt was a girl-next-door type; Grifasi, a roughneck corporal. The Public Broadcasting System (PBS) liked the production enough to film it for their "Theater in America" series, and the four friends were thrilled with this additional exposure.

But they paid for it in naiveté. The Playhouse Theater was on the "wrong side" of Eighth Avenue, the side of the street where men didn't shave until late in the day and women were either too fat from the starches of poverty or too thin from drugs. It was a real New York scene, one that was alien to these suburban-reared kids. The first day of rehearsals tested their mettle. "I'm a compulsively early arrival," says Miss Hurt, "so I went round the corner to a bodega and ordered some coffee. And the storekeeper says to me, 'You workeen thees street?' I said yeah, and he said, 'Well, I see you some tine.'

"Then I realized what he thought, and I said, 'No, no, I mean I work around the corner.' but it was too late. So I said, 'Omigod,' and I paid for the coffee and got out of there.

"When I told Meryl, she said, 'You drink too much coffee.' She had a straight face. Then she hugged me and said, 'I'll protect you.' We were like little kids acting like big ones."

They were also reveling in the new excitement of professional work. When that Phoenix season ended, the group couldn't wait to get together for the next one. It was an opportunity that afforded young actors a chance to grow together in various productions. Yet some crushing news sapped their enthusiasm. Soon after the season was over, it was announced that it had been the Phoenix's last one as a repertory company.

"That was one of the best groups of young actors ever gotten together," says Miss Hurt. Meryl agrees. She ascribes the failure of the Phoenix repertory to "money—the ins and outs of institutional financing." But the women had a plan. The men were in on it, too. In the future, when they were old-old—"like fifty-five," says Meryl, they'd form a repertory company of their own.

It was a close friendship, one that actors could enjoy only after they developed mutual trust. That was a difficult proposition for a group of actors professionally pitted against one another. They were often competing for the same parts. They all needed the money. And most important, they all needed to be seen on stage. But they made a pact to avoid jealousies and applaud loudly for one another. On slow days, they talked about their methods—none at all really, they just loved to bring language to life. So they read voraciously: new plays, obscure classics, *Variety*. They spent hours drinking cheap wine in Greenwich Village, on the Upper West Side, and in the area around Little Italy that would soon, unfathomably, become chic. They were an odd lot, these four kids: Grifasi, a bold-featured show-off; brown-haired Mary Beth Hurt, still asked for an ID card at bars because she looked so young; lanky, gawky Lithgow; and Meryl, a WASP with angles. They didn't dress well. Their apartments were furnished with relatives' castoffs and bare light bulbs. Each of their beds was, at one time, only a mattress on the floor. And they couldn't have cared less. All that mattered were rehearsals and long runs.

When Meryl got a small part in a movie called *Julia*, they toasted her success and listened for the melodious sound of a cash register ringing. Each of them heard it. Not only would Meryl be able to buy a real bed, and some bookcases, maybe, but this movie, this source of manna from heaven, was a "truly worthy endeavor."

Based on a semi-autobiographical vignette in Lillian Hellman's best-selling *Pentimento*, the film was about the friendship between two women, a friendship observed, said the author, over time. Meryl especially loved Hellman's definition of the title *Pentimento*:

47

Old paint on canvas, as it ages, sometimes becomes transparent. When that happens it is possible, in some pictures, to see the original lines: a tree will show through a woman's dress, a child makes way for a dog. . . . That is called pentimento because the painter "repented," changed his mind. This is all I mean.

About the people in her story, she said, "The paint has aged now and I wanted to see what was there for me once, what is there for me now."

Meryl played Anne-Marie Travers, a flirtatious, intelligent social butterfly who grew up in the South with the main protagonists, Julia (Vanessa Redgrave) and Lillian Hellman (Jane Fonda). After high school, the three lose touch. Miss Hellman becomes a successful playwright in America, Julia a freedom fighter in Europe, and Miss Travers an international gadabout. Meryl's part was small but important: she functioned as the unwitting go-between.

When she flew to London for filming under the direction of Fred Zinnemann, Meryl was so nervous she broke out in hives on the first day. "It was just being in the presence of Jane Fonda, Vanessa Redgrave, and Jason Robards," she says. But she hated the black wig she was forced to wear and the insipid lines she had to deliver. "I come in and out of scenes and say, 'Julia says,' and then 'What do you think of that?' I wear red in every scene and I look bizarre."

She landed another small part in another story about friendship: the TV version of Wendy Wasserstein's *Uncommon Women and Others*, originally performed at the Phoenix Theater. Meryl was the only newcomer to the TV production, taking over Glenn Close's stage role. In the story about Mount Holyoke graduates who reminisce seven years later about their time at the exclusive school, Meryl played Leilah, the unhappy graduate who is planning to move to Iraq to escape the competitive system and the constant overshadowing by her former roomate, played by Jill Eikenberry. Her experiences at Vassar, like Mount Holyoke one of the elite Seven Sisters schools, helped her develop the character. During rehearsals and filming, she became close to her costars, a coterie of serious young actresses on the rise: Swoosie Kurtz, Ellen Parker, Cynthia Herman, Anna Levine, Ann McDonough, Alma Cuervo, and Miss Eikenberry. Meryl's part may have been the smallest, but again she'd eclipse these peers in a matter of months.

She and Miss Hurt and the other Phoenix Theater gang saw less of one another after Joseph Papp called Meryl on Christmas Eve and invited her to rejoin the New York Shakespeare Festival for its summer operation at the Delacorte Theater in Central Park.

"Joe got on the phone and asked: 'How would you like to play a fanatic nun?' I said 'I'll have to check my book.' No, no, I said yes immediately," Meryl says.

Actually, he was inviting her to take two parts. In the first half of the summer, before playing Isabella in *Measure for Measure*, she'd perform Princess Katherine in *Henry V*.

At that time, she addressed the issue of American actors doing Shakespearean plays. "I envy the British the wealth of experience they can call on, but we have a different tradition in America. It's called heart and guts," she told them. "Besides, I can't miss what I never had." Then she got down to work.

She learned Katherine quickly so that she could begin performing her at night while rehearsing Isabella during the day. It was a crazy, challenging schedule. "Pure madness, but I loved it," she admits. Nightly, at about midnight, she'd call Miss Hurt or Grifasi and rave about her good fortune.

"One of the things in Shakespeare is that the character is fully realized in the words," she says. "You find yourself in the play through the words. There's no middleman. Then you serve the poetry. Your obligation is to the verse, then the meaning comes through."

Meryl worried the production wouldn't find an audience. "It's so hard for a 1976 audience to sit back and believe that purity of the soul is all that really matters to Isabella," she said during rehearsals. "That's really hard for them to buy." But then she found a little of herself in the woman: "She's dogmatic, has a great consistency. She's very sure of herself. Then she finds her emotions make demands on her convictions," Meryl added, presaging her own actions.

While acting the "fanatic nun," attentive to the emotional shadings of the script, the meanings of the words blazed through Meryl. She realized she was in love with her costar.

He was Angelo, the Duke's choice to rid Vienna of vice. While executing his duties, including condemning Isabella's lascivious brother to death, he lusts after Meryl, the chaste virgin. In praising the production, Mel Gussow of *The New York Times* wrote: "We sense the sexual give-and-take between her and Angelo, and she also makes us aware of the character's awakening feelings of self-importance and power."

After the opening, the two went to a chic Chelsea spot, the silver, Art Deco Empire Diner, where they stared at each other. After several glasses of wine, they began to talk. Their life stories spilled out. The small restaurant wasn't big enough to contain them. They left, hitting all the lively spots on the Upper West Side, cramming a year's worth of dates into a single evening.

And then they went to bed.

Meryl awakened with a hangover and red eyes. She felt wonderful.

Her Angelo was still asleep. His name was John Cazale.

8

ACTING NURSE

Hollywood has a short, selective memory when it comes to Michael Cimino. Before he made the disastrous $36.5 million *Heaven's Gate* in 1979, the small, wiry director was being touted as the big new force in film. Some said he had the best instincts around.

Cimino exercised his gut feelings in 1977 when he asked Meryl and Cazale to act in *The Deer Hunter*. Like a pair of vaudevillians about to get a shot at national acclaim, they couldn't quite believe their good fortune. In their small West 69th Street apartment, messy with strewn clothes, fast-food containers, and marked-up copies of Shakespeare, Strindberg, and Chekhov, Streep and Cazale called themselves "roommate thespians."

"They were so happy, it was so apparent, I felt they could do anything," says Al Pacino, Cazale's acting partner in *The Godfather*, *The Godfather Part II*, and *Dog Day Afternoon*.

By the time Cimino needed their answers, their stimulating, crazy life was coming apart with the specter of death. The lethargy that had bothered Cazale for a few months had finally been diagnosed as cancer.

Cazale was honest with Cimino. "I'm undergoing treatment," he told the young director. "But I can understand if you have to back down." Cimino didn't need time to think. He'd stick with Cazale. Meryl started to cry. It was a mixed-up kind of weeping in which joy and sorrow were thrown together. She'd have another chance to act with Cazale—but it would be her last.

Shooting on what was to become the epic movie about the horrific impact of Vietnam on small-town America was postponed from March to June. The fear that Cazale would grow worse made the waiting unbearable. Before shooting began, Meryl threw herself into theater roles as if she could stave off the inevitability of Cazale's death by acting out different endings. Peter Turner, a production assistant at Lincoln Center's Vivian Beaumont Theater, remembers "this driven blonde running with several different scripts into the various rehearsal halls muttering lines from each. 'Who is that?' I asked the casting director. She gave me this all-knowing grin and said, 'That's Meryl Streep and she's going places.'"

Coming to grips with Cazale's impending death aged Meryl, but she was still a giddy, often silly, young actress who became tongue-tied in the presence of stage greats. But that same self-effacing charm also landed her a choice role.

In 1976, she won a Tony nomination for her part in *27 Wagons Full of Cotton*. The awards breakfast was held at the Regency Hotel. She and Mary Beth Hurt "got there very early," says Meryl. "We knew it would be packed with luminaries.

"I had just seen Irene Worth in *Sweet Bird of Youth*, and I collared Arvin Brown [the director] before the breakfast and I said to him, 'You gotta introduce me to Irene Worth.'"

The room was knee-to-elbow with celebrities. "It was so star-studded," says Meryl, "that Mary Beth and I immediately went to the ladies' room and started smoking.

"Finally, Arvin knocked on the door and said, 'Come out of there—I've got Irene.'"

The eggs were getting cold. The bacon had shriveled. The mimosas had turned tepid. Meryl emerged from the bathroom and began to gush. "Your performance in *Sweet Bird* has provided me with enough inspiration for a lifetime," she told Miss Worth, who proceeded to compliment Meryl on her performance.

"What do you plan to do in December?" Miss Worth asked.

"Unemployment, I guess," Meryl said.

"Fine," said Miss Worth. "Think about *The Cherry Orchard*."

Mary Beth Hurt got a part in the Chekhov play, too. She played the aristocratic Anya to Meryl's lovesick, flighty maid, Dunyasha.

They shared a dressing room backstage at the Vivian Beaumont, where they acted more like boarding school roommates than rising young stars. Miss Hurt usually got dressed and made up first since her part required more elaborate costuming. Meryl sat and lounged and puffed. They were as different as Jack Spratt and his wife. When old friends dropped by, Meryl held up two identical handkerchiefs. "This," she said, "is the difference between Mary Beth Hurt and me."

The handkerchiefs, embossed with big red cherries, were gifts from Irene Worth to commemorate the opening of *The Cherry Orchard*. Miss Hurt's hankie was as crisp as a nurse's uniform. Meryl's, on the other hand, looked like it had been fished from the bottom of a crowded trunk. It was as wrinkled as an elephant.

But unorthodox director Andrei Serban wasn't concerned about Meryl's sloppy habits. It was her face that intrigued him. He chose Meryl for *The Cherry Orchard* because of "the bones in her face. And she takes well to direction," he adds.

Life in the theater provided Meryl with respite from the exigencies of nursing Cazale. She could even joke about illness with Miss Hurt. They both suffered from minor cases of eczema. "It's such a disgusting disease," they agreed. "Not at all romantic like TB." They had just discovered Susan Sontag's book-length essay *Illness as Metaphor*, in which the feminist intellectual discussed why consumptives, including the poet Byron, were romanticized in their day. However much Meryl disdained fashion trends, intellectual pretenses had exerted a strong appeal for her ever since her Vassar days. And *Illness as Metaphor* held special meaning for Meryl. Miss Sontag was also suffering from cancer. Cazale's predicament was never off her mind.

After long rehearsals, she'd hurry home to entertain him by imitating the imperious Serban. Cazale encouraged her "Lucille Ball tendencies." He also brought out her impish nature. Standing ramrod straight, her hair in a messy bun, her arms flailing, she'd impersonate the Rumanian director while Cazale rested on an old sofa. "Falling down verrry verrry funny," she'd yell in Serban's serious voice. Cazale would laugh. And she'd fall down just as she did when Serban directed her.

There were always extra characters in their small apartment. Meryl could mimic Zsa Zsa Gabor; the local bag lady; the low, dulcet tones of Irene Worth; and a host of serious, overbaked young actors. Meryl would summon them from inside herself to dispel the gloom in their small, ill-lit apartment. It was a high-minded amateur hour: Meryl desperately wanted her acting talents to heal Cazale.

Her life was split between acting and taking care of Cazale. She had little time, or inclination, for big parties. After expending so much energy on frivolous pursuits in high school, Meryl was thereafter fearful of wasting time.

Mary Louise Streep

Meryl   Bernardsville
Pretty blonde . . . vivacious cheer-
leader . . . our homecoming queen
. . . Many talents . . . Where the
boys are.
Gymnastics Club 1, 2, 3, 4; French
Club. Sec. 1; J.V. Cheerleader 2;
Varsity Cheerleader 3, 4; Chorus
1, 2; V. Pres. 3, Pres. 4; Class
Treas. 1; Crimson 3; Bernardian
Art Editor 4; Morning Announcer
3; Quill and Scroll. V. Pres. 4;
Girls' State 3; Jr. Prom Comm. 3;
Intramurals 1, 2, 3; Homecoming
Queen, 4; Natl. Honor Soc. 4.

Above: Senior photo.
The Bernardian '67

Right: Homecoming
Queen. *The Bernardian
'67*

Below: Her girlhood
home in Bernardsville,
New Jersey.

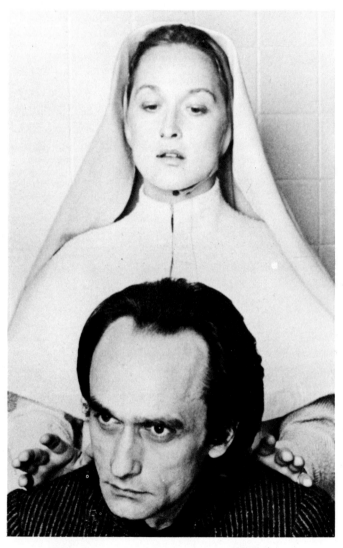

With John Cazale in *Measure for Measure,* at the Delacorte
Theater in Central Park, 1976. (Frederic Ohringer)

Dancing with Robert De Niro in *The Deer Hunter*. (Universal)

The radical lesbian feminist arguing with her estranged husband, Woody Allen, in *Manhattan*. (United Artists)

With her senator lover, played by Alan Alda, in *The Seduction of Joe Tynan*. (Universal)

Left: With husband, Donald Gummer, 1979. (Paul Schumach, Metropolitan Photo Service, Inc.)

Opposite: Before the separation in *Kramer vs. Kramer,* with Dustin Hoffman and Justin Henry. (Columbia)

With Dustin Hoffman and their Oscars for *Kramer vs. Kramer.* (Wide World Photos, Inc.)

Feeding author, and co-host, Norman Mailer at a media party, 1979. (Adam Scull, *New York Post*)

With the man who is obsessed with her, played by Jeremy Irons, in *The French Lieutenant's Woman.* (United Artists)

With Irons as they play the parts of the star-crossed lovers in the modern-day scenes of *The French Lieutenant's Woman*. (United Artists)

Left to right, Meryl, Dr. Helen Caldicott, and Jill Clayburgh at a nuclear disarmament fundraiser, 1982. (Mark Vodofsky, *New York Post*)

Left to right, Peter MacNicol, Meryl, and Kevin Kline on their Brooklyn rooftop in *Sophie's Choice*. (Universal)

Meryl, Kurt Russell, and Cher in the plutonium factory in *Silkwood*. (20th Century-Fox)

Acting offered immediate rewards. For her performance in *The Cherry Orchard*, Meryl received rave reviews. Walter Kerr of *The New York Times* found her "brilliantly funny." But the play itself was panned by other reviewers, who complained of "distortion by design" and "heavy-handed symbolism."

Three days before its limited run was over, Meryl took on another project, this time a lead. When Shirley Knight dropped out of *The Happy End* during previews, Meryl was invited to replace her in the Brecht-Weill collaboration.

She credits her Yale buddy, Joe Grifasi, with getting her the part. "He knew I could sing," Meryl says, "and he'd say to me, 'You should do Lil,' and then he'd say to the director [Robert Kalfin], 'Meryl could do Lil.' So I got to do that part that way."

When the chamber musical first opened in Berlin in 1929, it was greeted by hisses and catcalls. Upon its opening at the Brooklyn Academy of Music in 1977, the *New York Post*'s Martin Gottfried said: "The show is plainly jinxed."

And it was.

Anything that did go right was deemed an act of God's good-will. Meryl's hasty recruitment for the play left her with only three days to memorize the part of Hallelujah Lil, a Salvation Army lass out to reform a beer-swilling rake. Luckily, she was familiar with the part, which she'd played during her graduate school days at Yale. But this time around there was new blocking and a modified libretto. Working feverishly, she got it down. Then, a day before its formal opening, leading man Christopher Lloyd fell onstage and ripped two ligaments in his right leg. His cast extended from ankle to hip.

"I don't even care if she still remembered some of her lines from Yale," says Lloyd's understudy, Bob Gunton. "It was an astounding lesson in concentration for me. Here I was going into a part that I'd already worked on, and I was more nervous than she."

But Meryl remembers the opening night differently. "I felt like I was stepping out on a diving board at the World Trade Center," she says.

A month later, on the night before *The Happy End* moved to Broadway, Gunton came down with measles and Lloyd hobbled onstage in his place.

What else could go wrong? The cast was hysterical with possibilities. "It was as if we were earmarked for disaster," says choreographer Patricia Birch, the tiny dynamo who had worked on *Grease*. "And we wanted to prove we could conquer it all. So we intentionally set traps for one another."

Meryl took no part in the good-natured pranks. She was frightened. She had been exposed to measles and feared she could infect Cazale. At her urging, Dr. Max Kamen gave the whole cast gamma globulin shots. The vaccinations couldn't prevent the illness, but they did offer a greater chance of immunity. Just a chance. Meryl was reaching for the last straw.

Illness adds a heightened urgency to life. While Cazale was sick, he and Meryl lived and relived only the good times. After she left *The Happy End* in June, she and her lover spent quiet evenings reading to each other, cooking pasta, and walking through "their park," Central Park, the site of their first joint acting triumph.

Ironically, it had been in Shakespeare's darkest comedy, *Measure for Measure*. In it, Meryl as Isabella staunchly defended her virginity against Cazale's salivating Angelo. "More than our brother is our chastity," she admonished him in the play. When they fell in love for real, they defied the immortal words day after day.

9

THE DEER HUNTER

Flying off to Ohio for *The Deer Hunter* that summer cut into their private world, but their acting life gave them another universe to enjoy.

"Some actors feel humiliated by costumes," says Karel Reisz, who directed Meryl in *The French Lieutenant's Woman*. Meryl feels liberated by them." Cazale, say his contemporaries, was the same way. The trouble was, Cimino had barely begun to concoct the story that would give them a new life.

All Meryl knew about her part was that she'd play an ordinary young naif, the proverbial girl back home. It didn't immediately engage her imagination. Yet she would do anything to work with Cazale.

"I was ecstatic to be in *The Deer Hunter* because I was living with John Cazale at the time, and we could be in it together," she recalls. "That is so hard for actors, you know, you're always in different cities, missing each other. . . . They needed a girl between two guys in the movie and I was it."

Little did she know that what she had signed for was, in

Cimino's words, "just a notion." She was accustomed to acting on stage in revered dramas where even the omission of a single word could bring on fits of apoplexy from directors. Meryl's only other screen experience had been the bit part in Lillian Hellman's *Julia*. And playwright Hellman was another stickler for the written word.

The experience with Cimino taught Meryl an important lesson: Hollywood lives and dies on its instincts. EMI, the British-based company that financed *The Deer Hunter*, had also agreed to get involved on a hunch. Cimino told its executives a story. Nothing was written down. And they came aboard immediately. "*The Deer Hunter* was like Michael's novel," Meryl says. "They allowed him to unfold his story as he wanted to." She was right. Cimino was shocked.

"They said, 'Okay, do it,' " Cimino recalls. "I said, 'What do you mean do it?' They said, 'Do it.' I asked, 'When?' They said, 'Forthwith.' I asked, 'What does that mean?' They said, 'Yesterday.'

The company put up $7.5 million. Cimino was scared. It had been four years since his last movie, *Thunderbolt and Lightfoot*. "You know, people just forget who you are," he says. "Four years and all that work and nothing. Francis [Ford Coppola] had already begun work on *Apocalypse Now*; all the other Vietnam movies were finished or nearing completion. I had this terrible feeling I had let everything slip by."

The frenetic fight against the clock was about to begin. Cimino had a script to deliver. Cazale was fighting to live. And even before Cimino had finished her character, Meryl was practicing Linda's personality: vulnerable, sweet, supportive, passive. It was the way she always prepared, looking for the heart of the character before assuming the flesh and bones. Linda was quite a challenge for a woman known for her quiet determination. "Oh boyyyyy," Meryl wondered to a friend, "how am I gonna stand up for this character?"

Cimino toiled night and day. He wrote in cars and buses and jet planes, with Derek Washburn lending his seasoned hand to the screenplay. At the same time, Cimino was also scouting film locations. "It was a terrible way to work," he says now, "but there were no alternatives."

The filming delay gave Cimino more time to travel in Thailand to research the scenes that were supposed to take place in Vietnam. He scaled Mount Baker in the state of Washington for the deer-hunting scenes. He and *The Deer Hunter*'s star, Robert De Niro, visited as many grimy steel towns as America had to offer to pick up the look and feel of working-class life. The pair walked the main streets, visited the mills, downed brewskies in bars, and traded stories in VA hospitals. They discovered Chuck Aspergen, who played Axel in the movie, on the job, working for U.S. Steel in Gary, Indiana.

The whole cast and crew met in Mingo Junction, Ohio, where extras were dressed in flannel shirts, heavy parkas, woolen gloves, and hats in ninety-degree temperatures. The postponement caused one drawback that nobody anticipated. The late-fall setting had to be shot at the height of summer.

Chuck Aspergen remembers everything about his first movie, but especially Meryl and Cazale. They were "always together," he says. "Some of us thought they were married. But they weren't big stars to me, not like De Niro. They kind of kept to themselves. John seemed to be limping. I thought the heat had gotten to him."

The cancer had spread to Cazale's bones. He was dying in the middle of a tiny steel town that symbolized the kind of pain one just grins and bears. The place would become Clairton in the movie. It was just the right working-class, Middle American setting for Cimino's vision of "hometown." It would become the town where Vietnam left its numbing sting on those who went and those who stayed behind. De Niro, Christopher Walken, and John Savage served their country and suffered in the movie. Streep and Cazale were both left at home. Their psychic pain, in a way, was greater. It was visible in the unrelenting terrain of Mingo Junction: the black and gray of an overworked town.

"I would never suggest that the geography or visual environment of the film is more important than what's going on with the people, but it's a major factor in getting the right tone," Cimino insists. They traveled to other cities: Cleveland, Ohio; Weirton, West Virginia; Duquesne, Pennsylvania. "Intuition plays a big part in finding something special," Cimino told the overworked cast and crew.

Not everybody was buying creativity spewing forth from the mouth of this director. While other directors, from Alfred Hitchcock to Steven Spielberg, have been given creative freedom on their films, here was Cimino, a relatively unknown director paid to be a functionary of the studio, the producer, and the star, making a movie without a clear-cut idea of where it would go. "Nobody knew exactly what was going on," says Walken. "But still we all had the feeling this was going to be a big one."

That kind of excitement bred dedication. But just as things were beginning to run smoothly, Cimino got a call from a frightened executive at EMI. He said Cazale had been given the standard physical required of actors before they shoot a movie. The doctor's report was in. Cazale, it said, was dying of cancer. Therefore Cazale was out.

"I told him he was crazy. I told him we were going to shoot the movie in the morning and that this would wreck the company. I was told that unless I got rid of John, he would shut down the picture. It was awful. I spent hours on the phone, yelling and screaming and fighting," says Cimino. Tears welled up in his bassett-hound eyes. There'd be a lot of tears shed during the making of *The Deer Hunter*.

"Then I was told I had to write an alternative script in

case John died. And he wanted to see exactly how I was going to write John out. I called a psychiatrist I know and asked him what I should do. I called this guy back at EMI and explained that I would tell John what I was doing; then the guy said he had to be there when I told John. I asked why. He said, 'How will I know if you really told him?' Well, I went insane. I screamed, 'You mean after all this, you don't trust me?'

"I told him that not only was I not going to tell John but I was not going to write an alternate script and he could shut down the film for all I cared, and I slammed down the phone."

Meryl sensed what was going on, but she could do little. It was one of the only times in her early career she wished she was a big star with the kind of power that makes people listen. Instead, she turned on the eerie composure that would always serve her well, as she and Cazale toured the heartland: towns called Struthers, Steubenville, Follonsbee. They were learning what made America tick. And in the process, they learned a little about themselves as well. If Cazale were to be axed, Meryl would leave the picture with him.

Cimino was about to pack it in, too. "This was the first time since I have been involved in making movies that I thought, 'I'm getting out. I can't do this. It is not worth it, talking about life and death like this.'"

Miraculously, EMI backed down. Filming began in earnest.

Meryl had come a long way in defining her character, the patient grocery store clerk who waits for Christopher Walken to return from Vietnam, only to realize her attraction to his close friend, Robert De Niro.

How did she manage to imbue such an ordinary woman with so much soul? By picking her brain for role models. "I know a lot of girls like that, who didn't question their lives," says Meryl. "Knew them in Jersey. They're waiters. Wait to be asked for a date, wait to be asked to marry, wait for their boyfriends to come home from war. Never move on their own. They can't. But they're worthy of notice. They're waiting to live."

The paradoxical underpinnings were beginning to show. Meryl had never waited to live, and now she was fighting hard so that someone else could. Robert De Niro remembers her antic sense of humor when the oppressive heat on the set forced her to use a blow dryer to whisk away the sweat. "Women who are very beautiful often let their beauty inhibit them," he says. "They tend to have no character. When a woman is beautiful and has that extra edge—like Meryl—it's nice."

During shooting, actor George Dzundza's sideburns kept falling off. Meryl would imitate someone caught naked. "She has," says De Niro, "an excellent sense of timing and she's very funny. She has a sense of herself as being funny. She was always around getting people to laugh."

But when Cazale was in danger on the set, she avoided visiting. After months of negotiations with U.S. Steel, Cimino was given permission to bring his cast and crew into the Central Blast Furnace in Cleveland. The floor of the blast furnace is a place of unbelievable heat where molten metal, fired up to 3,000 degrees, flows like water. Steelworkers have nicknamed the spot the "widow maker." Cazale and the others played their roles as the tap hole of the furnace was unplugged and the molten metal spewed forth. Meryl wasn't around.

"The flames made us look translucent," John Savage recalls. "Everybody looked like ghosts." It was good Meryl wasn't there. She had been fighting the idea of ghosts throughout the movie. And for a brief period while Cazale was in remission, it looked as though they both were winning.

The victory was a false one. Toward the end of shooting, Cazale's condition grew worse. He became so weak, he could barely speak his lines. He realized he was dying.

Meryl tutored herself in optimism. She would have pleased her fondest admirers, those who praise her ability to become, imperceptibly, the character she's portraying. Some even doubt she's acting at all. In her best performances, she blurs the fine line between fiction and reality. She makes miracles.

Alan J. Pakula, who directed Meryl in *Sophie's Choice*, witnessed her uncanny ability at transformation. "That kind of talent," he told the *New York Post*'s Jerry Tallmer, "is a mystery. In Salem, that kind of acting could have got you . . ." Pakula couldn't finish the sentence.

"Burned as a witch?" suggested Tallmer.

"Yes," Pakula agreed.

Call her a witch, an angel. Whatever she had, she used, and her best performance would be for Cazale. For him, she swallowed the attributes of hope—smiles, trust, good cheer, faith—and she became confident that his condition would improve.

10

A TIME TO MOURN

When they returned to New York, Cazale entered Sloan-Kettering Memorial Hospital on an out-patient basis for a series of cobalt treatments and chemotherapy. Soon after, Meryl had to leave for Austria. Shooting on *Holocaust* was about to begin.

One consolation in the difficult parting was that she'd be acting with her friend Michael Moriarty. They'd played together before in Meryl's first New York play. *The Playboy of Seville*, and also her first TV drama, *The Deadliest Season*. She had accepted the latter part, as Moriarty's wife, because "it was offered." For a young actress to have the opportunity to be viewed by millions of people was also an enticement. Money, too, was a factor. Her off-Broadway roles, however lauded, sometimes paid as little as eighty dollars a week. Naturally, Broadway paid more. In the 1970's, scale salary was about $500 a week. But money, however much she needed it, was never a deciding factor when Meryl took a role.

The biggest benefit of *The Deadliest Season* was that it would please Meryl's parents. Although Harry II and Mary

Louise made an effort to see most of her theatrical debuts, they were at heart suburban homebodies who liked nothing more than curling up in comfortable chairs around the set after dinner to watch something good. And they thought *The Deadliest Season* was great.

So did the critics. When it first aired over NBC in March 1977, John J. O'Connor of *The New York Times* extended lavish praise on this dramatic indictment of the savagery in hockey. "At a time when television is being seriously and widely questioned about its own violent content, *The Deadliest Season* is an especially noteworthy presentation for a major network," he wrote. "Beyond that, this is an exceptionally impressive production."

Moriarty remembers Meryl as being "especially nervous on the set. She'd bite her fingers and twirl her hair. I liked her, though. Anybody who was putting that kind of effort into a TV movie was a serious player. And she was just getting her feet wet."

Her part was small. Meryl played Sharon, the loving spouse of Moriarty, a professional hockey player who is pressured into provoking brutal fights on the ice to increase the excitement of the game. Like *The Deer Hunter*, its target audience was men. But this was still television, where subtlety is more feared than sex. Meryl was forced to utter lines that thudded harder than a fall on the ice. Still, she made them work.

"When I watched you in a game it turned me on," she tells Moriarty. Her delivery is quiet and slow, as if she is searching for better words to tell her husband that she loves him. When she can't come up with them, the effect is poignant. She turns a stock character into a heroine.

Herbert Brodkin, producer of *The Deadliest Season*, was so impressed with Moriarty and Meryl he cast them together again in his controversial miniseries, *Holocaust*. But this time, they were adversaries.

Set against the background of Nazi Germany, *Holocaust* tells the story of two families, the Dorfs and the Weisses. Moriarty played Eric Dorf, a young, unemployed lawyer whose wife convinces him to join the SS, where he quickly becomes one of the most indomitable of Nazi persecutors. Meryl played a Roman Catholic, Inga Helms, who marries a Jew, Karl Weiss, and loyally follows him to the concentration camps.

The irony was deadly. Here she was playing a woman whose husband was being tortured, while Cazale lay dying at home. But Meryl remained stalwart. "There was," says co-star Fritz Weaver, who played Meryl's father-in-law, "not a moment of self-pity."

It was a turning point in Meryl's career. She achieved instant fame when the nine-and-a-half hour series aired. And she hated it. She had had misgivings about the subject from the start. The Holocaust was a historic fact of such monstrous proportions that, in Meryl's view, it might well be unsuitable for dramatic scrutiny.

"It was something surreal," Meryl recalled soon after it was shown on four consecutive evenings in April 1978. "I was riding my bike through Chelsea one day when these four guys in a Volkswagen started yelling out the window, 'Hey, Holocaust, hey, Holocaust!' Can you imagine? It's absurd that that episode in history can be reduced to people screaming out of car windows at an actress."

When Emmy time came around, she declined to pick up her statuette. It was delivered to her later, only to accumulate dust on a warped shelf in her apartment. In the teleplay, Meryl was the only German worth redeeming during the whole series, other than an infirm old priest who eventually died in Dachau. "I was so noble, it was sickening," she says.

Scholars, too, had mixed feelings about *Holocaust* and they debated its merits in respected journals. "As a TV production, the film is an insult to those who perished and those who survived," wrote Holocaust survivor Elie Wiesel. "Too much, far too much, happens to one particular family and too much evil is perpetrated by one particular Nazi officer."

Meryl's unhappiness with her part was magnified by missing Cazale during the shooting. She couldn't appreciate the postcard beauty of Austria because she spent most of her offscreen hours worrying about him.

"It was grim," she recalls. "Austria was unrelentingly Austrian. The material was unrelentingly grim. My character was unrelentingly noble. Mauthausen was too much for me." Survivors of that camp, a final destination for many men and women who had been beaten and tortured at other sites, remember the inexorable horror of the spot. It was the eleventh concentration camp for Moishe Feurstein, a New Yorker who was reminded of his awful past by the TV drama. "They had us with no clothes on. People walking around, you could see through them. Skeletons they had everywhere," he says. "Naked bodies piled up to the ceiling. Some dead, some alive, who knew?"

And the awful memories lingered in subtle ways that would turn Meryl's stomach. Around the corner from the filming site in Mauthausen, there was a hofbrau that in the evenings would fill with retired German soldiers. "When the soldiers got drunk enough, and it was late enough," Meryl says, "they would pull out their souvenirs of war; it was very weird and kinky. I was going crazy. John was sick and I wanted to be with him."

Why, then, did she agree to the role? "I did it for the money," she says. It was one of the very few times she compromised her principles. At home, the hospital bills were getting out of hand.

Cazale was lingering. When Meryl returned, the hospital bed made his body seem even more frail. He had lost nearly thirty pounds. The painkillers put him in and out of touch. Through sympathy and empathy, Meryl could feel his pain. And she finally wished it were over.

He died on that warm Sunday night in March, before the release of *The Deer Hunter*. He was forty-two, with the bulk of what promised to be an auspicious career ahead of him. His widowed mother Cecilia, his sister Catherine Benjamin, and his brother Stephen conducted a private service for him in Winchester, Massachusetts.

A time to mourn. A time to weep. It was Meryl's time. She was devastated by Cazale's death, "emotionally blitzed," in her words. Even though she had sensed it coming, she could not accept the final moment. There is no way to prepare for death, and Meryl purposely didn't. She fought for Cazale's life as much as he did. But like her character in *The Deer Hunter*, who waited and waited for her man to come home, Meryl, too, went on with life when Cazale was lost to her.

"John's death is still very much with me," she says now. "It affects everything that happens afterwards. But just as a child does, I think you can assimilate the pain and go on without making an obsession of it."

11

THE SEDUCTION SCENE

Living alone in the apartment she'd shared with Cazale
left Meryl feeling overwhelmingly despondent. Her
loss was magnified by the silence. She'd walk from
the kitchen to the living room to the bedroom, expecting to
find him. Her brother Third moved in with her to see that
she ate, got dressed, took walks. Her family was worried.
She had refused to back out of a movie commitment. Three
weeks after Cazale's death, Meryl was scheduled to begin
work on *The Seduction of Joe Tynan*. Her part called for cool
detachment. While she was packing for herself and trying to
sort out Cazale's possessions, that stranger rang the bell—the
woman from California who had the apartment lease that she
and Cazale had signed several years earlier. Meryl, consider-
ably unnerved, was left without a home.

Third's college chum, Don Gummer, invited Meryl to
move her belongings temporarily into his Soho loft. She
dropped off a few pieces of furniture, her books, and some
articles of clothing she never wore but couldn't bear to give
away. Then she left for Washington to begin the movie.

Everything happened so quickly she has vague memories of the time. "It was a selfish period, a period of healing for me," she says. "I was trying to incorporate what had happened into my life. I wanted to find a place where I could carry it forever and still function." The work didn't ease the pain, but it did save Meryl from further despondency. She credits Alan Alda, who wrote the screenplay and starred as Tynan, with helping her through "that awful period. The whole film crew, too. They were amazingly supportive."

"We were all worried about her," says director Jerry Schatzberg. "I thought the movie might be too much so soon after all she'd been through. But I was wrong, I'm happy to say."

Meryl played Southern civil rights attorney Karen Traynor, a woman whose marriage to a corporate workaholic leads her to have an affair with Alda, a senator and presidential contender. She discussed the similarities between politics and acting with Melvyn Douglas, the actor who married Helen Gahagan, a former actress who had served as a congresswoman from California. "They're very similar worlds," Douglas told Meryl. "That's why there are a lot of single actors," she quipped. Only a month after he died, Meryl had already begun to view her life without Cazale.

"I did that film on automatic pilot," she says about the movie, the story of what happens to presidential yearnings when corporal desires get in the way. "But it was probably the best kind of therapy because I worked so hard that there was no time to think of anything else."

Schatzberg is noted for working his actors hard. The compact, gray-haired former fashion photographer has the proper dose of excess energy that film producers love. Meryl, however, was used to a more leisurely pace. "At night when we finished shooting, I just collapsed into bed and fell asleep," she says.

Blanche Baker, Carroll Baker's beautiful blonde daughter, first worked with Meryl on *Holocaust*. She found a different woman on the set of *Joe Tynan*. "She was in mourning," Miss Baker recalls. "We all felt for her. I often wondered how she could do the love scenes." Miss Baker, who played Alda's rebellious daughter in the movie, remembers one scene where Meryl had some difficulties. A particular love scene between Meryl and Alda called for a lot of playfulness. They were required to rip each other's clothes off, more in the spirit of good fun than high passion. "She carried it off," says Miss Baker. But by the end of it, Meryl was dripping with nervous perspiration.

Alda confirms that the scene was an ordeal for Meryl. "But she came through," he says. "She looked at the movie as some kind of a test, a test she had to pass. She was determined not to buckle."

There were many light moments as well. Onscreen, she had fun with her character, borrowing her Louisiana accent from Dinah Shore. "You know," Meryl says, mimicking Miss Shore, "see the U.S.A., in your Chevrolet."

As soon as a full crew began shooting exterior shots of the House of Representatives, the Senate, and the White House, Washington's power brokers were curious about *The Seduction of Joe Tynan*. Rumor travels faster in the nation's capital than in any other city in the United States. Pages on their lunch breaks, lobbyists at embassy parties, and under-secretaries of state all had theories about the real model for Joe Tynan.

"It caused quite a fuss at the time," says Alda about his first screenplay. "But the fuss was good advance publicity, right?" The guessing game also took Meryl's mind off Cazale.

The real fun came with further intrigue. All that was revealed about the movie was its moral: lust can jeopardize political careers. Some Washington bigwigs assumed it must be based on Jimmy Carter, who talked about his own lustful thoughts in the notorious 1976 interview the President gave to *Playboy* magazine.

As soon as Washington found out that Meryl was playing Alda's lover, they looked for a counterpart in Carter's life. The loose talk traveled all the way to the White House. After the movie was edited, the president was one of the first people to request it for a private screening at 1600 Pennsylvania Avenue.

He had fewer worries compared to a certain dashing senator from Massachusetts. When filming began in Baltimore and Annapolis, gossips went on a field trip. They noted that the liberal-leaning senator played by Alda wore half glasses on the end of his nose and bore an uncanny resemblance to Ted Kennedy. Then they whispered some more about which paramour Meryl could be playing.

Alda insisted he wrote the movie with no one public figure in mind. "Basically, it's about workaholics," he says. "There's an immense cost to being successful. Sometimes, you lose out on the important things in life. Sometimes, you spread yourself too thin."

The same feeling touched a chord in Meryl's own life. She was beginning to scout around for a lasting set of priorities. At the top of her list: the need to begin anew. She wanted to start her own family.

Meryl returned to New York with a sense of accomplishment. The odds were against her finishing the movie, and not only had she completed it, but also she had again made her character live and breathe. During the final days of shooting, Schatzberg took her aside. "You were shrewd, glowing, witty," he told her. "You're my ideal Southern belle."

When the movie opened a year later, Kathleen Carroll of the *Daily News* predicted Meryl "has what it takes to become a major star." Rex Reed wrote: "She conquers the screen with honey dripping off her fangs as she provides Joe Tynan with . . . a sexual awakening that turns him from a lovable lunk to a lascivious lover." Her screen conquest would soon be followed by a more important one.

12

SOHO SHREW

Soho is a place where bohemians dress like businessmen and businessmen dress like bohemians. The pandemonium in its narrow streets—all styles of the epochs in Manhattan's history bumping into one another—was just the change of pace Meryl needed after Cazale's death. She moved into Don Gummer's loft on Soho's Franklin Street after filming *The Seduction of Joe Tynan*, just as Gummer was leaving for Europe.

She first got to know Gummer—the man she had no idea she would shortly marry—through his decor. Meryl liked his disregard for material possessions—the old couch, the battered kitchen utensils. Here was an artist who took his vocation seriously. Her own increasingly obsessive desire to protect her private life was mirrored in Gummer's secluded, unpretentious home. Before they even began a relationship, Meryl realized she had found a soul mate: a man who, like her, valued isolation and work.

His own huge wooden sculptures filled the studio area of the apartment and spilled out into the living quarters. The neighborhood was comfortably pleasant, too. He lived off lower Broadway on the edge of fashionable Soho. Artists and small businessmen, with odd little factories that manufactured pipes and buttons and cigarette papers, peaceably coexisted. The area was quiet except for roaring trucks at night, the city's peculiar lullaby.

"I started to write Don while he was away," Meryl recalls. "He and my brother had been friends for years and I had met Don two or three times, but I honestly didn't remember him. We really got to know each other through our letters."

Their transatlantic correspondence proved they had a lot in common. Both Meryl and Gummer were well-educated, with loving families who supported their artistic endeavors. Each, however, refused financial help; both felt a great need to make it on their own. Meryl listened to Gummer's advice. "The only way you can do your best," he wrote Meryl, "is to be involved with the best." Soon after, she realized she needed the stimulus of live theater. After a year away, Meryl needed to go back to her spiritual home.

The timing was perfect. Joseph Papp called her in the spring of 1978 to do *The Taming of the Shrew* with his New York Shakespeare Festival that summer. After a short but well-deserved break at her parents' retirement home in Mystic, Connecticut, Meryl began rehearsals. "With TV films and movies, I haven't done a play in over a year," she said at the time. "I needed very much to come back to the theater." It was all there for her: the exhilaration of daily rehearsals, the opportunity to tune and hone a sentence or a phrase so that it worked on many different levels, and the quiet, thinking camaraderie of stage actors.

When acting in a film, Meryl felt no sense of the intellect at work. She admitted that filming bored her. "Those long waits between takes. There's nothing like a curtain that rises at eight and comes down at eleven. You give of yourself."

The Taming of the Shrew flooded her with memories of the time she'd acted in another Shakespearean comedy and had fallen in love with her costar. The rehearsal halls on Lafayette Street in Greenwich Village were the same ones she and Cazale would rush to when their intimate conversations made them lose sense of time. The costumes came from the same room. The play would again be performed outdoors at Central Park's Delacorte Theater, near the Upper West Side apartment she'd shared with Cazale.

Her *Taming of the Shrew* costar, Raul Julia, had to dispel the ghost from Meryl's past. "I was another person," he says. "A different kind of actor." But Meryl knew that; she'd acted before with Julia in *The Cherry Orchard*. Together in *Taming* as Petruchio and Kate, he and Meryl forged a revolutionary interpretation of Shakespeare's most misunderstood play, using love, not power, as the overriding motivation for their domestic difficulties.

Director Wilford Leach conducted long rehearsals that turned into marathon workshops. Actors practiced their lines while costumers and set designers milled around getting a feel for the production. It was a happy circus where everyone got the chance to play the clown. Inside, Meryl was still in pain. But her demeanor belied her sadness. During the grueling, rewarding, sessions, Meryl often stole the show with her behind-the-scene antics. The boys in the back row in high school had taught her well.

During rehearsals, just looking at her could make the technicians and stagehands hysterical. Sitting on a high stool, Meryl would hike up Kate's skirts thigh-high to reveal two incongruously red kneepads, her protection against the frequent tumbles she would endure.

One day in August, the distraction proved too much for Julia. The tall, handsome actor couldn't concentrate on his lines. "She *swings* as sweetly as the nightingale," he recited quickly, in the staccato tone reserved for rehearsals.

Observers tried to stifle their laughter. Julia fell silent. Then he began a litany of Spanish curses ending with "*Jesucristo!*" He jumped from his stool. "Sings! Sings! Sings!" He knocked his head with two fists as if to beat the word in place. "She sings as sweetly as the nightingale!"

Meryl pounced on a chance for a little improvisation to relieve the tedium. She began tapping her fingers, swaying to imaginary music, literally swinging, and, at the same time, also typifying a cool chick, a swinger.

Julia took her lead and began a furious flamenco dance. For sheer style, it would have been difficult for the two of them to match their improvisation with an equally brilliant rehearsed bit.

Leach called for a break. Their stunts pointed out to the director that his stars were under stress, trying to come up with a solution to the antifeminism inherent in the play.

During rehearsals, pandemonium often reigns with paranoia close at its heels. The director has one idea, the actor another, but sometimes the stagehand comes up with the best solution. In this case, Leach didn't have a clue. He wondered aloud why he chose the play in the first place. He was sure bands of roving feminists would show up every night during performances and hiss. To try to defend its sentiments, during the height of female militancy, was next to impossible.

It was Meryl who proved to Leach his choice was a good one. Like a dutiful enlisted man who leads the troops out of the foxhole, she showed Leach it took bravery to get to the heart of the play. As she often does, Meryl theorized her way through the predicament. "Feminists tend to see this play as a one-way ticket for the man, but Petruchio really gives a great deal," she told her director. Scholars might be shocked at her conclusion, but it worked for her purposes. She found a way to live with the subservient Kate without compromising her own principles and, more importantly, without modifying the text.

"It's a vile distortion of the play," she continued, "to ever have him striking her. Shakespeare doesn't do it, so why impose it? This is not a sado-masochist show. What Petruchio does is bring a sense of verve and love to somebody who is mean and angry. He's one of those Shakespearean men who walk in from another town. They always know more, see through things. He helps take all that passion and put it in a more lovely place."

It was Cazale she was thinking of when she described Petruchio. They had discovered each other in much the same way. Some people find parallels in the Bible to make sense of their lives. Meryl turned to Shakespeare.

"That jerk," she said in loving tones about Cazale during rehearsal, "made everything mean something. Such good judgment, such uncluttered thoughts. 'You don't need this,' he'd say, 'you don't need that.' Kind of like Petruchio: What's right stands alone." Kind of like Gummer, too, whom she'd marry in less than a month.

Rehearsal started up again. Although the problem of antifeminism was solved on a theoretical level, it still had to be woven into the text. The clowning continued. "How tame when men and women are alone," Julia recited. "A meek wretch can make the curstest shrew. Give me your hand, Kate!" Coyly, Meryl extended her left foot. It was time for another break.

They discussed the thorniest problem in the play: Kate's final speech, when she vows to love, honor, and obey. Julia suggested he give the speech instead. "I could say the same thing about my duty to her. Maybe it was more appropriate to give that speech to women in Shakespeare's time. But I can see it being done that way someday. Kate gets up and says, 'Petruchio, tell these men what duty they do owe their wives.' And I would get up and do it myself," he said.

Meryl couldn't fathom tampering with the Bard. Besides, she'd found no problem with the speech. "What I'm saying is I'll do anything for this man," she argued. "Look, would there be any hang-up if this were a mother talking about her son? So why is selflessness here wrong? Service is the only thing that's important about love. Everybody is worrying about 'losing yourself'—all this narcissism. Duty. We can't stand that idea now either. It has the real ugly slave-driving connotation. But duty might be a suit of armor you put on to fight for your love."

Julia watched her. She became reflective. She had lived the duty she defined so well when she nursed Cazale. He knew what she was thinking. They would remain close friends, each supporting the other in times of sorrow. Without a word, she extended her right foot to Julia. This time he kissed it.

Actress Holland Taylor, who had attended Meryl's opening night in Central Park, called her performance of Kate "Mozartian." But the real music sounded just after the show closed when Meryl married Donald Gummer.

As soon as Gummer returned from his European jaunt, "He built me a little room in his loft, and told me I could stay," Meryl says. "And twenty minutes later, we got married!" She was joking. Actually, their live-in courtship lasted two months.

Although her father had always advised Meryl "to play the field," he was delighted by the wedding. Both parents had known Gummer for five years as Third's "nice friend who raided the refrigerator." The wedding was held on a warm September day in the backyard of the house in Connecticut. It was attended by their families (Gummer has five brothers), and a few close friends. After the short ceremony, they fled to Maine for a four-day honeymoon.

"We were all shocked by the haste of their marriage," says an artist friend of Gummer's. "It seemed to come out of the blue. I mean, I thought he was still living with that other woman."

"That other woman," the strikingly attractive dancer and choreographer, was shocked by Gummer's change of heart. "It's past history now," she admits. "But I'm still not over the way it was over. It took me a long time to come to terms with [the break-up]. Strangely enough, it's worse for me now. There are repercussions all the time. I see their names in the paper. I have to deal with their presence in my life every time I pass a movie house," she says.

It was Meryl's fame more than Gummer's that was irksome to the dancer. After the marriage, "Gummer sort of dropped out of the art scene for a while," says a Yale classmate. "It was a combination of things. Tastes had changed. Nobody really went for his formalist, cerebral, strict sculptures anymore. He wasn't the new hot fashion. In my opinion, he was less of an artist then. When he latched on to Meryl, the stuff became boring." As Meryl's star rose, Gummer's dimmed somewhat.

13

THE STRUGGLE TO FIND MRS. KRAMER

Kramer vs. Kramer would make any attempt at avoiding celebrity a lost cause for Meryl. Paradoxically, she had to work hard to land the part that would imprint her face on the public's mind forever, a situation she later deemed "excessive hype." Columbia Pictures had already signed Dustin Hoffman—one of the biggest box-office draws of his generation—for the part of Ted, the rising advertising executive who loses his wife only to rediscover himself and his son.

The studio was not about to risk giving the part to Meryl. She may have received critical attention onstage in New York, but her part in *Julia* was just a walk-on and both *The Deer Hunter* and *The Seduction of Joe Tynan* had yet to be released when casting for *Kramer vs. Kramer* began. All the studio knew about those pictures was that Meryl didn't have the leads. Sure, she had stunned audiences by her talent in *Holocaust*, but in mogul parlance, "That was this character thing on TV. I mean, the box is so small, who remembers?" In their thinking, Meryl was not yet a bankable enough commodity to play Hoffman's wife, Joanna.

81

They were after Kate Jackson, the dark-haired star of "Charlie's Angels," and they nearly had a deal sewn up with her to play opposite Hoffman. Producer Stanley Jaffe, writer-director Robert Benton, and Hoffman himself agreed to audition Meryl for the small part of Phyllis the lawyer, the attractive woman who beds down with Hoffman and, while in the buff, meets his young son, Billy.

Four days after her wedding, Meryl went to see them. Benton and Hoffman were hooked. They turned to Jaffe: "She's perfect," they said. "But for the part of Joanna."

When she got the part, the news moved quickly through the lunch crowds at Ma Maison on the West Coast. In New York, movie executives dining at the Russian Tea Room, Le Cirque, and La Côte Basque put down their forks, picked up their cigars, and talked about the coup pulled off by that strange-looking dame, what's her name? "They called me Strep," Meryl says. "It was less creepy than Streep."

Meryl was pleased for one reason alone. Because the movie executives had embraced her, they'd have to accept her artistic input. Their faith gave her leverage. For the first time, Meryl decided to fight to do her part her way.

Her stubborn streak resurfaced. There was no way she'd play Joanna the way the character was written in Avery Corman's novel, the basis for the movie. "They couldn't have not changed the script!" she says. "I mean, I couldn't have been interested in the role if they hadn't changed the script!"

At another meeting attended by the three men, Meryl outlined her objections. There were quite a few. Columbia wouldn't be easily persuaded to scratch any of Corman's words; after all, they had spent $200,000 to buy the novel. It was a long afternoon, the kind when big shots revert to their childhood and wish for a fire drill—anything—to escape.

"This is what is wrong with the story," she began, and proceeded to rip apart the character of Joanna Kramer, a woman who leaves her husband and six-year-old son when the pressures of career and home prove too much. Meryl said the woman was "too evil," her conflicts "too narrowly described." She talked about the "identifiable problems" raised by the contemporary dilemma, but said Joanna "doesn't reflect them sympathetically enough."

Benton remembers her "earnestness" that day. "She was elucidating concerns we all had. But she gave them words. 'We never understand why she walked out,' Meryl told the moviemakers. "It was true. So we listened," he says. "And she became the real Mrs. Kramer."

Her role was still "the heavy." How can a mother who deserts her child elicit any sympathy? Meryl managed to get her point across by sheer will. "There's a very interesting filmic device that's used," she recalls. "A lot of what other characters do and say has to do with me, but I'm really there only at the beginning and at the end. It's like a person who walks out of the room, and everybody tries to explain why she did what she did, and finally, after they've agreed on some version of things, she comes back and explains it herself. I'm set up as a villain, so I like the idea of reappearing and trying to turn that around."

Her relatively short time on the screen didn't prevent Meryl from immersing herself in her character. She wanted to think like Joanna so that she could feel like her. She reached out to her mother first. Mary Louise Streep has always worked as a commercial artist, but for much of her married life she did her work at home. Many of her New Jersey friends were housewives, though. Could they relate to such a contemporary villainess? Mrs. Streep shocked Meryl when she said: "All my friends at one point or another wanted to throw up their hands and leave and see if there was another way of doing their lives."

The idea of a wife abandoning a family still sent shock waves through Middle America; it was worse than being a harlot. But if her mother's friends had entertained the idea, Meryl assumed it must have at least crossed the minds of other women. She began to read magazines aimed at middle-class women. The stories disheartened her. "Every month, they carried the same story," she says. "'Judge Mary So-and-So, brilliant jurist and mother of five, handles her career and this amazing household, together, terrific!' Everything this woman reads tells her that she must be able to do both! But what if you can't do both? What if you just can't handle it? What if you can't understand why the world won't allow you to do one or the other?"

Meryl became a sociologist in an unfamiliar terrain: Manhattan's Upper East Side. She window-shopped along Madison Avenue; peeked into beauty salons; hung out at Bloomingdale's. Strains of Brahms wafted into crowds of shoppers. The musicians were Juilliard students who crossed town from their West Side haunts for an easier buck. Some Upper East Siders even threw silver dollars into their proffered hats. But once the privileged of Park Avenue got home, they became prisoners of their penthouses. That's what Meryl deduced. In a Central Park playground off Fifth Avenue, she watched young mothers push their children on swings. She eavesdropped on their conversations.

They never dreamed married life would be this way, they said to one another. Whether they had household help or not, it was the same daily routine. Cleaning (or instructing someone to clean); dinner at eight, kids in bed by nine—the deadly humdrumness of it all. And then the larger concerns: He doesn't like his job, but he can't get another one in a different field at his age and we couldn't live without a salary for even one week and I never worked long enough to carve out a career and what happens, anyway, if some morning after I find his clean shirt he gets run over by a car? Meryl listened, and she began her process towards empathy.

Sex was another big topic at the playground. We never

want it at the same time, the mothers would begin. I don't want it, he wants it. Sometimes I think he wants it because I don't want it. And then I think I'm crazy, or just tired, and I say okay and we do it and I feel worse, because afterward I know I didn't want it.

"The more I thought about it," Meryl says, "the more I felt the sensual reason for Joanna's leaving, the emotional reasons, the ones that aren't attached to logic. Joanna's daddy took care of her. Her college took care of her. Then Ted took care of her. Suddenly, she just felt incapable of caring for herself."

She saw Joanna Kramer as a muddled, unhappy woman on the brink of a nervous breakdown she knew would never come. It was the angst of an upper-middle-class woman in a Burberry raincoat who'd just as soon be naked. She walks out on her child because she has nothing left to give him.

In public statements Meryl says, "I always felt that I can do anything." But the private Meryl is often beset by periods of self-doubt. That's just the point—these two sides of her surfaced as Joanna Kramer. Meryl had enough confidence to take on what was deemed an unsympathetic role and cause audiences to weep for her. Some of them even took her side. Benton's wife, Sally, was so impressed with the daily rushes, she wanted her husband to "rewrite the end and give Meryl custody of the kid."

All this advance praise for Meryl, who was, in fact, only the supporting lead in the movie, caused Hoffman to balk. Would she have the gall to upstage him? She was using tactics Hoffman himself had relied on to exert his influence.

Because she was onscreen so little, Meryl needed all the ammunition she could muster to deliver her lines the way she interpreted them. And when the lines rang a false note, she changed them. Hoffman was flabbergasted.

They had some "bad fights," Hoffman recalls. She spoke negatively about his character to the press. "He's the prototypical seventies person," she said about Ted Kramer, "and you just can't *stand* him! But Dustin makes him so funny—as a high, high-pressure, real finger-popping, fast-talking guy, somebody who has an answer for everything. He's so unneurotic in a way, and yet when you see the way he has to behave to make a living, it's horrible."

During the restaurant scene where Meryl announces she will seek custody of their son, Meryl wanted to rewrite the dialogue. Hoffman was sure the reason was to upstage him. He became so enraged he threw a wine glass against the wall. Shooting stopped while they argued. "I hated her guts," he says.

Meryl wanted to break the news late in the conversation, instead of at the beginning, as it was written. Benton was willing to try the change. Hoffman was not. "Someone as obsessed as Dustin creates a lot of tension and puts a tremendous burden on the people he works with," Benton says. But after a lengthy disagreement, Meryl won Hoffman over. "Yes, I hated her guts," he says, "but I respected her." Hoffman realized she "was not fighting for herself, but for the scene. She sticks with her guns and doesn't let anyone mess with her when she thinks she's right."

There were other problems. The script called for the feuding couple to push and pull for the attentions of little Justin Henry, who played their adorable screen son, Billy. They vied for his loyalty off-camera as well. During a break in filming the playground scene—Billy sees his Mommy after a long absence, only to be chased by his Daddy too—Hoffman tried to win popularity points. "Who do you really want to live with?" Hoffman asked Justin. He pointed to Meryl. "Her!" shrieked Henry. "She's nicer." The entire crew started to laugh.

"Oh, yeah?" replied Hoffman. "Work with her five weeks and then see what you say."

A month later, near the end of shooting, Hoffman begrudgingly offered signs of respect for Meryl. "She'll work twenty hours a day," he said. "She's an ox when it comes to acting. She eats work for breakfast. It's like playing with Billie Jean King. She keeps trying to hit the perfect ball."

The way Benton tells it, the penultimate sequence in the movie pushed Meryl over the top from beatification to sainthood. Again, she was dissatisfied. This time she felt the courtroom speech in which she outlined her reasons for leaving her family was too flimsy. Meryl totally rewrote her lines.

"I thought, oh my God," Benton recalls. "I'm going to lose two days' work. One, rewriting what she's done, and the other, soothing her wounded feelings. Well, the scene was brilliant. I cut only two lines. What you see there is hers."

Filming her testimony took all day, eight or ten tedious takes, in close-ups, long shots, medium shots. "She stayed at the same level all day long," Benton recalls. "She was so good, she devastated us." In the scene, she trembles and twists with the nervous determination that she is right. In that moment, she walks away with the picture.

For the final take, the cameras zoomed in on Hoffman. Meryl had only to speak her lines for his reaction shot. "The whole crew had its back to Meryl," the director remembers. "When it was finished, we turned around and there was Meryl in tears. She'd given that much just for a reaction shot."

The real Meryl Streep is just as acute an observer. She likes nothing more than to don an old sweat shirt and walk the streets, watching ordinary people go about their business. She stores away their little unconscious gestures and intonations for future use in acting roles. Her friendships are also of the undemanding variety—a phone call out of the blue, a spur-of-the moment invitation for drinks. She does not enjoy staged events in her personal life.

When Benton announced he was throwing a wrap party

for *Kramer vs. Kramer*, he had to beg Meryl to go. The festivities took place at a chic Upper East Side spot called La Boîte. When Meryl arrived, wall-to-wall photographers hovered near the entrance. But on December 11, 1978, they couldn't care less about Meryl. She slipped in virtually unnoticed. The papparazzi, including their king, Ron Galella, and his probable successor to the throne, David McGough, were after one person only: Dustin Hoffman.

He was used to the cat-and-mouse games celebrities played with the press. Hoffman entered the restaurant through the kitchen and stayed there, talking to the chef, for nearly half the party. Meryl exchanged pleasantries with Hoffman's then-wife, dancer Anne Byrne. Gummer ate canapés. It was so quiet a party that Justin Henry fell asleep on a banquette with Hoffman's daughter Jennifer.

Meryl watched them snore: legs entangled, mouths agape. Their world wasn't complicated yet. It was just a huge uncharted territory offering new discoveries every day. Meryl wanted a role that would offer her the same kind of wonderment.

"You can literally do anything," Benton told her before she went home.

14

THROUGH THE LOOKING GLASS

Meryl's roles literally became curiouser and curiouser. In 1978, at age twenty-nine, she became Alice in Wonderland in Elizabeth Swados's musical version, *Alice in Concert*, at Papp's Public Theater. Romping onstage in lavender overalls, she was the image of a precocious child. She sang onstage for the first time since high school, twenty-nine songs in all. She rolled around, played with her hair, sucked an occasional thumb, bounced up and down. "Just like she did when she was a little girl," says her mother. "She's still like a child," says her friend Liz Swados. "So full of surprises. With her, it's constant Christmas."

Meryl took the part of tiny Alice, the girl who tries to make sense of Lewis Carroll's delightfully crazy characters, because "I had just done three movies and I needed to jump and leap. All I wanted was to forget the way I look, to become unselfconscious, to have the freedom children have when they're doing something in the middle of a roomful of adults looking at them—and they just totally don't care." It was Meryl's way of getting reacquainted with her own spontaneity.

And the critics, like guests at the Mad Hatter's tea party, drank it up and asked for seconds. Because Papp decided the show wasn't ready—"I saw two run-throughs and felt it was at an impasse," he says—it played for only three days. The critics took what they felt was an injustice and made it into a cause célèbre.

"This is a mature actress who has reinvented herself as a magical, ageless child," wrote Mel Gussow in *The New York Times*. "By the end of the concert we are convinced that Alice is tall, blonde, and lovely—just like Meryl Streep.

"Miss Streep has a small voice, but a pure one, and she uses it to its best advantage, alternately singing and talking. . . . Miss Streep's enchanting performance deserves a full, resplendent production."

In the *New York Post*, Marilyn Stasio wrote: "Meryl Streep was born to play Alice . . . but we'll never have the pleasure of seeing her in the role, if the New York Shakespeare Festival doesn't get shaking—quick. . . . On many occasions, Joe Papp has flourished the charm of the White Rabbit. Why can't he make a little magic now and pull something out of his hat?"

According to Papp, the project was "suspended. There's no question," he said at the time, "that I'm doing this show." Meryl, too, wanted to see it return. "Liz has a great idea," Meryl said after it closed. "She said wouldn't it be wonderful if Alice could really be Alice and pop out of a rabbit hole every once in a while and just be there for all to see and hear. Then disappear back into the hole and hopefully pop up someplace else at some other time. It sounds marvelous."

Along with the disappointment of *Alice*, Meryl received a greater blow when she discovered what was going on with *The Deer Hunter*, Cazale's last picture. After entrusting Cimino with thirteen million dollars, nearly double what he first requested to make the movie, the producers felt there was no audience for it. They sat on it and waited. "They were concerned about everything," Cimino recalls. "The subject, the violence, the length. They always acknowledged that there was something there. They couldn't deny their own reactions. But to a large measure in this country we've lost confidence in our intuition. We rely too much on information, on data."

Enter Allan Carr, a rival producer best known for his outrageous caftans and his $100 million box-office film success, *Grease*. In July 1978, he sat all alone in an 1,100-seat theater at a private screening of *The Deer Hunter* and wept his way through the three-hour movie.

"By the time it was half over, I was so emotionally undone, I was crying. I felt I was seeing a genuine masterpiece. Everybody, Bobby De Niro, Walken, Savage, Meryl Streep, the kid from *The Godfather* [John Cazale], they were so good. It's not the kind of picture I could make, but I could appreciate it."

His idea was to bring the picture out for a limited run over Christmas so that it would be eligible for the Academy Awards. "At every Christmas cocktail party in New York, people would be asking each other if they had been able to get into one of eight performances of *The Deer Hunter*. The New York syndrome is if you can't get into something, it becomes special," Carr says. "Then we'd bring the picture back when the Academy nominations were announced. On a piece of paper that day in July, I wrote '9 to 11 nominations.'"

The picture received nine nominations. Among them was Meryl's first.

15

PAPP

When it comes to success off Broadway, there's really only one producer worth mentioning. He paces in his office, a large vaulted room painted yellow with a three-foot-tall satin pink flamingo in the corner, and still manages to overshadow the decor, even while talking about dull things. Single-handedly, this disheveled man changed the course of theatrical history when one of his small workshop productions moved from Greenwich Village to Broadway. Once it traveled uptown, *A Chorus Line* never left. It became the longest-running musical in the history of the Great White Way.

But Joseph Papp—producer, director, singer, fundraiser, and the first serious contender to the throne of impresario Mike Todd—refuses to rest on his success. He's out there scouting for material, and actors to bring it to life.

One of his finds was Meryl Streep. Another was Thomas Babe. They came together in the summer of 1978.

On the face of it, the period was a dark one for Papp. To the outrage of the New York theatrical community, he closed *Alice in Concert*. But that play's untimely death at the

Public Theater may have been, in part, the result of his un-
qualified enthusiasm for another project, Thomas Babe's
Taken in Marriage.

While *Alice* was in rehearsals in the summer of 1978,
Babe arranged for a reading of his play to be given at the
Public's Newman stage. Meryl and Elizabeth Wilson, rehearsing *Alice* on another Public stage, gladly agreed to participate. All her working life, Meryl has delighted in discov-
ering new playwrights, different voices for her to speak.
Babe's good friend Dixie Carter, already cast as the entertaining stripper, aptly named Dixie in the play, joined the
two women in the impromptu reading for Papp.

When you hear something good onstage, it doesn't matter if there are props or costumes or scenery. As Papp himself says: "All you need are two planks and a passion." The
passion made its presence felt that afternoon. "We were all
kind of tired," recalls Miss Wilson. "Especially Meryl." Papp
heard something else in their voices and in the playwright's
words: a wrenching, ordinary truth. He stood up in the middle of the reading and said, "I'm going to produce this."
Meryl and Miss Wilson were shocked. "He never does that,"
says Miss Wilson.

"I was knocked out," Papp says. "I thought it was
Babe's best work. His earlier work was extremely verbal, and
he's such a wise guy, he conceals emotions. But here, he'd
found it. It's a play of tremendous female, human energy and
it's extremely understanding of women." Meryl and Miss
Wilson were asked to join the production on the spot.

The show would give Meryl, who'd been married less
than six months, the chance to be with the girls again; that
lovely, carefree time when secrets are shared, problems are
solved, and common ground is discovered. When Kathleen
Quinlan and Colleen Dewhurst joined the cast, Meryl felt as
if four instant best briends had dropped from heaven.

The nature of Babe's drama encouraged close connections. If a group is playing a family gathered in a church hall on the eve of a wedding, each of its members is going to want to get to know the others offstage.

Meryl describes her part as someone "very Upper East Sidey." Having already finished *Kramer vs. Kramer* no doubt helped her characterization, as did friendships with Vassar girls much like her sophisticated character.

Papp and director Robert Ackerman sat in the audience during rehearsals, drinking black coffee and keeping quiet. They marveled at the actresses' ability to unearth their characters. The women joked among themselves, and teased one another. They immediately assumed an unspoken camaraderie, like old friends. One day Meryl walked across the stage and fell. The men thought she was kidding. Elizabeth Wilson rushed to her aid. "Don't worry about me," Meryl said. "I always fall down. I fall in just about every play I've been in, it seems!" After all the women rubbed her knee like a roomful of concerned grandmothers, she bounced right back to work, and continued to trip.

Meryl was Andrea, sister of bride-to-be Kathleen Quinlan, daughter of mother Colleen Dewhurst, niece of Elizabeth Wilson, and no friend at all to Dixie Carter, a stripper type who was hired by the menfolk—offstage characters—to show up as a practical joke.

Waiting for the men to arrive, the female family members passed the time onstage revealing little insecurities and hurts. When there was little left to jaw about, Dixie encouraged them to dance. She led the way with a sexy strut. Miss Dewhurst shook in place. Miss Wilson swayed. Bride-to-be Quinlan did a jig. And Meryl, the most self-possessed of the lot, stiffly, awkwardly moved her feet in a tight pattern of despair. The dances were a stroke of genius. They revealed more about the women than their words. It was the inspired choreography of Meryl's brother Third that set the women in motion. Meryl, naturally, helped get him the job.

Reviewers were again charmed by her talents. "Meryl Streep, as Andrea, is a series of prisms, breaking the character's pale light into flashes of misery, remorse, frustrated love, self-hatred," wrote Richard Eder of *The New York Times*. "Beautiful, self-possessed, with a brittle laugh and brooding eyes, she is the most wretched member of the family."

Said Clive Barnes of the *New York Post*: "Meryl Streep, with an Afghan hound look and a voice like a cultivated buzz-saw, is the personification of toneless elegance."

But it didn't come easily. Elizabeth Wilson remembers Meryl's stage fright. "When she's onstage, there's a look in her eye of a real fighter," says Miss Wilson. "But though you don't see it when she's performing, Meryl suffers greatly before an opening. She perspires. She paces. I don't know if she actually gets sick, but she's very, very nervous—more so than almost anyone I've ever known.

"She would say to me, 'I wonder why people are afraid to be onstage,'" Miss Wilson recalls. "So I'd tell her stories about actresses I'm close to who'd say, 'I'm so scared, I'm so afraid I'm going to lose control onstage, I'm going to die there.'

"And Meryl said, 'Lizzie, do you believe that?' And I said, 'Yes.' The look on her face then was so terribly sad. I was sorry I told her." The pressure of constant success placed Meryl in a kind of limbo. She fully expected to fail. And since she had never received a bad review, the prospect of being trashed in print was devastating. She became paralyzed. Her narrow world was closing in.

When you've risen to celebrity status in five short years, when producers say you can play any role, when your only method is to become the character you're playing and you're not even sure how you do it, paranoia finds an easy target. Even if she didn't fail, someone would inevitably say Meryl did.

"I'm sure that everybody's chomping at the bit to do that," Meryl said. "It's because of all the glowing, gushing things that have been said. And I'm standing in the middle of this: one pours flowers on me, the other one sees that, so now it's time to dump the shit."

Meryl decided to escape the limelight—the excitement of opening nights when she couldn't breathe until after the curtain came down, the interminable wait for reviews to be read, the feelings of guilt when she was the only one to get good notices, and the phone calls from agents and interviewers pining to talk with "the hottest actress since Jane Fonda," as she is known in the trade.

Soon after *Taken in Marriage* began rehearsals, she and Gummer conceived their first child on a cold January night in their eclectic Soho loft. She thought she wanted to be an ordinary mother-to-be, the kind who knits baby booties, craves pickles and ice cream, and hunts for bassinets.

But the traditional concerns left her cold. She wanted a baby, yes, but she was an actress who wanted a baby. It was the first time she realized her career had colored so much of what she was.

"Thank God Don is a creative person," Meryl says about her husband. "He understands my need to work."

Says Gummer: "She's learned how to look at objects and I've learned how to look at people. There are many different levels of love. Ours is founded on a very deep-rooted feeling of trust. We're best friends."

The demands of Meryl's career would test their friendship—and their love.

16

MAKING WAVES, AND BABIES

The pool at the Beverly Hills Hotel is made for loung-
ing. Producers and young starlets gather in late
morning for the ritual of seeing and being seen. The
older men wear trunks with matching print jackets. The vir-
ile sorts force their forms into tiny, colorful, satiny briefs.
But the women all dress alike: skimpy bikinis incongruously
accented by thick gold chains, dangling diamond earrings,
gold and silver stiletto-heeled sandals. Everybody drinks
Bloodys or Perriers splashed with vodka and lime, and waits
for something to happen.

When Meryl and Gummer flew out to Los Angeles,
something happened. In the first week of April 1979, they
arrived at the Beverly Hills Hotel to prepare for the Academy Awards show on April 9.

In the midst of this poolside circus, the greatest show on
earth, Meryl emerges from her room, walks purposefully to
the edge of the pool, and dives in. Her splash aches in the
ears of Hollywood's movers and shakers sitting on their butts
in the hot sun. Who has the audacity to swim in the pool?

They look up. There is Meryl, in the center ring, wearing an old tank suit.

And Meryl swims twenty laps.

What prompted Meryl to participate in an affair for which she had so much disdain?

She went because of John Cazale. Her first Oscar nomination, for the supporting actress role in *The Deer Hunter*, was for the movie closest to her heart. Picture her weeping in a movie theater. She has seen the film "six or seven times," she recalls. At each viewing, "It broke my heart, seeing John." Meryl viewed the movie as a chance to see her lover live onscreen as the unpredictable, headstrong outsider, the friend who set his buddies on edge. Her presence at the awards that night was a tribute to him. Had she won that night over Maggie Smith, who received the award for *California Suite*, Meryl would have dedicated her acceptance speech to Cazale, the actor's actor who didn't live long enough for the public to get to know him.

Getting dressed for her first Academy Awards ceremony had made her nervous. There would be 300 million viewers watching her. She tried on several outfits and nothing looked right. Those who caught a glimpse of Meryl that night when the cameras panned the star-studded room noticed a retiring woman with little makeup dressed in a simple suburban party dress. She clutched her husband's arm. Her hair was loose, flowing like a college girl's. Nobody could equate this simple image with the overpowering effect Meryl left when she was acting. It was as though a different person, a smaller shadow of the blazing screen Meryl, showed up that night.

The staff at the Beverly Hills Hotel where she stayed during Oscar week didn't recognize her. In fact, they wondered who she was—this wide-eyed, silly blonde who gawked at celebrities.

She would again unknowingly send shock waves

through her professional community when she blasted Woody Allen, the informal dean of successful, intelligent filmmakers—a writer, director, and actor whose every utterance is analyzed, footnoted, and finally committed to memory. "Did you hear what Woody's up to?" is the kind of a line bound to turn heads in Elaine's, his favorite restaurant. If overheard by the bistro's formidable proprietress, it might cause Elaine Kaufman to favor its speaker with a choice front-room table. Knowing Woody had that kind of power.

A few weeks after her infamous debut at the Beverly Hills Hotel, Meryl made a more serious faux pas. After Allen's *Manhattan* opened on April 25, 1979, she proclaimed the bespectacled director "very self-involved. It's sad, because Woody has the potential to be America's Chekhov, but instead he's still caught up in the jet-set crowd type of life and trivializing his talent."

Who was this upstart actress passing judgment on the contemporary hero of the literati? After all, she had barely worked in the movie, admitting she doubted that "Woody Allen even remembers me."

In the movie, Meryl played Jill, Allen's former wife turned lesbian. She left her husband and, with their young son, moved in with her female lover. Then she wrote a best-seller called *Marriage, Divorce, and Selfhood*. The book had a devastating effect on Allen's screen persona. In one of the movie's scathingly funny lines, he summed up his feelings: "I believe in monogamy, like pigeons and Catholics." (In an odd way, Meryl would sincerely echo his lines in her own life. She approached her marriage to Gummer as an iron-clad commitment. She wanted to prove to the friends who scoffed at the haste of their courtship that she could make the marriage last forever. She would hide any troubles they might be having.)

But in Meryl's view, movie roles that didn't go right were proper grounds for open discussion. "On a certain level," she says about *Manhattan*, "the film offends me because it's about all these people whose sole concern is discussing their emotional states or neuroses," a state of affairs Meryl equates with heresy. In her restricted view, problems are trivialized when they are aired like dirty linen.

As soon as people began noting similarities between her small part in *Manhattan* and a real-life author, the controversy offended Meryl. A similar situation occurred during *The Seduction of Joe Tynan*, but in that movie nobody could figure out which real-life lawyer was used to form the basis for Meryl's character.

After *Manhattan* was released, New York–based writer Susan Braudy, a cofounder of *Ms.* magazine, accused Allen of borrowing the details of her life for his script. She charged Allen and cowriter Marshall Brickman with incorporating her curriculum vitae into the characters played by Meryl Streep and Diane Keaton. In actuality, Miss Braudy had written a compelling book called *Between Marriage and Divorce* about her break-up with Leo Braudy, a professor of film at several East Coast universities. In the movie, Meryl writes a book with a similar title and Miss Keaton is divorced from a college professor. Resemblances were far from identical, but there were just enough similarities to make everyone, including Meryl, a little nervous.

The connection seemed to be more than a matter of coincidence. While Allen and Brickman were preparing their script, Miss Braudy interviewed them for a long free-lance article she was doing for *The New York Times*. Instead, it appears, they did most of the grilling. "They made me feel so interesting," Miss Braudy recalls. "Especially when I was talking to Woody."

But she wasn't extremely upset by the movie, "just a little startled," she said. "Besides, I don't think those guys know too many girls."

Meryl knew differently. Woody Allen, she says from experience, "is very much a womanizer."

In the spring of 1979, her thoughts veered from her career to her family. Her first child wasn't due until November, but Meryl had a lot of catching up to do. She really hadn't had much experience with infants—no baby-sitting in high school, no relatives who'd talked about the enormous change a baby makes in a relationship. In February, she'd shocked her good buddy Joe Grifasi when she told him the happy news. After she attended his opening night in *Says I, Says He*—a controversial, scatological view of war-torn Northern Ireland at off-Broadway's Marymount Manhattan Theater—Grifasi was more interested in talking about the mysteries of birth than his own reviews.

"We wanted to have a child because not enough people in our circle of friends were having children," Meryl explained to Grifasi. "Friends of mine from college, who are very accomplished, are delaying children until they are older because of their careers."

Meryl's striking success gave her the luxury of temporarily halting her career for a baby. But on Grifasi's opening night, when the curtain rose on her friend and associate, she felt a tinge of regret that she wasn't onstage with him. Still, Meryl delighted in the knowledge that he was finally getting the critical attention she felt he deserved. *The New York Times* said: "Joe Grifasi's bitter, dry and inwardly turbulent Mick, refracts emotion into a burning pinpoint." It was the kind of praise often reserved for Meryl.

For the next several months, however, she had to content herself with the applause of a few friends in high-ceilinged lofts. Her only acting consisted of impromptu routines, like "Saturday Night Live" skits, that she'd developed with Grifasi. They performed willingly and often, in her living room or his.

101

By the time May arrived, Meryl was so bored she agreed to host her first public party. Again she was on new terrain, but cohosts Norman Mailer and International Creative Management (ICM) literary agent Lynn Nesbit introduced her to the wiles of party-giving with a purpose. The media bash was held in honor of the liberal weekly magazine *The Nation*. The press arrived in full force. Meryl provided them with a field day when she was observed feeding a piece of cake to Mailer in Miss Nesbit's living room. Mailer dispelled all rumors: "We have," he says, "something in common. We're both married to fine visual artists." An unspoken similarity, a difficult one, also held them together. Mailer and Meryl each outshone their mates, a situation that can encourage marital problems.

A week later, entertainment attorney L. Arnold Weissberger and agent Milton Goldman hosted a belated wedding celebration for Meryl and Gummer. Even the well-known guests were intrigued by the private couple. "They're adorable," said Tennessee Williams at the party. "It's hard for me to believe this sweet, shy thing portrayed my Flora [in *27 Wagons Full of Cotton*]." Douglas Fairbanks, Jr., toasted "the happy couple, for their marriage and their first edition"— Meryl's pregnancy was beginning to show. Familiar faces came out to congratulate her. Lucie Arnaz showed up with *The Elephant Man*'s Philip Anglim. Maureen Stapleton, Rosemary Harris, José Ferrer, Sidney Lumet, Michael Moriarty, Jean-Pierre Aumont, and the Joseph E. Levines all came to honor the union of an actress who had caused Hollywood to unleash its superlatives and her quiet, unassuming husband. They accepted Gummer because Meryl had chosen him.

Days later, Meryl and Gummer took their first European vacation together. She was anxious to get away from Hollywood types, but her agents convinced her to sail to England on an ocean liner. On the Queen Elizabeth II, Meryl caused a bigger stir than the ship's other famous passenger,

Louis Jourdan. She and Gummer rested on deck chairs, read aloud, relaxed, and avoided autograph hounds. They took tea and indulged in the midnight buffets. It was their first real vacation, a delayed honeymoon. Meryl thrived on the sea breezes and the chance to indulge in long, uninterrupted conversations with her husband. They talked about the responsibilities of rearing their baby and how they wanted to instill in their child a respect for nature and literature and learning.

When they returned, Meryl concerned herself with readying a space in the loft for her new child. She couldn't help but feel elated by her pregnancy. In the garden of a trendy restaurant, a svelte model handed out fliers for her boutique. Meryl joked with her. "Got anything in this size?" she asked.

Her pregnancy took up much of her day. In the mornings she read Dr. Spock, *Our Bodies, Ourselves*, and books on the Lamaze method of birth. Afternoons, she frequented Castle Clinton in Battery Park, where her husband had a thirty-five-foot sculpture on display. "It's a real big deal for him," she said at the time. It was one of his first shows since their marriage, and Meryl wanted to show her support.

In the evenings, she and Gummer took Lamaze natural-childbirth classes. Meryl was a quick study. She'd learned all about breathing from acting.

But the instruction turned out to be unnecessary. On Tuesday night, November 14, 1979, Gummer rushed his wife to New York Hospital. There, doctors discovered the delivery was to be a breech birth. They delivered the healthy, six-pound, fourteen-ounce boy by Caesarean section.

"There was nothing to it," Meryl says about giving birth to her first baby. "Don was with me and held the baby right after it was born. It seemed the most natural thing in the world." Although the baby was three weeks late, the couple had been counting on a girl so it took them a little while to come up with a boy's name. They decided on Henry, the old reliable moniker in Meryl's family, the given name of her father and brother. "We named him after Hank Aaron," Meryl joked a day after his birth. Then she realized the papers would pick up on her gag. "No," she quickly added, "it's just a good name."

As soon as Henry Gummer came home, Meryl nicknamed him Gippy. Like her own mother, Meryl realized a family name could become a burden in later years. And Meryl realized her son would have enough trouble as the child of a world-famous actress.

17

FIVE THOUSAND CHRISTMAS TREES

Gippy Gummer irrevocably changed his mother's life. With his birth, Meryl became as serious about her life as she was about the characters she portrayed.

The momentous change began with her wedding. "When you're single," she says, "you usually don't think twenty minutes ahead. But after you're married, you suddenly start thinking twenty years ahead."

The birth of her son caused her to further consider the future of the world. "This child will have to get us into the next century," she says. "His generation will have to deal with problems of survival that our generation never even thought of: pollution, depletion of natural resources, population control." With the birth of her first child, Meryl not only became serious about her own life, she became concerned with the idea of life. Gippy's birth politicized Meryl. She became an outspoken opponent of nuclear arms.

First and foremost, though, she was an actress. And in the year of her son's birth she was honored by her peers as never before. The National Board of Review cited Meryl for the three films she'd acted in that were released in 1979:

Manhattan, *The Seduction of Joe Tynan*, and *Kramer vs. Kramer*. The New York Film Critics Circle honored her for *The Seduction of Joe Tynan* and *Kramer vs. Kramer*; her performance in the latter also earned her a Golden Globe award and a Los Angeles Film Critics award. She picked up her first Oscar for *Kramer vs. Kramer*. At home, the bookshelf where she haphazardly displayed these awards was getting full. Praise trickled in from every corner of the world. "For a while there," she says with no pleasure, "it was either me or the Ayatollah on the covers of national magazines."

Harvard University's Hasty Pudding Club named her Woman of the Year. Grandpa Streep baby-sat with Gippy on the sidelines while Meryl paraded up Harvard Square, flanked by club members, who were dressed, in keeping with their 132-year tradition, in ball gowns and skirts. Meryl ribbed them about "their frivolous attitude toward women," and then joked that "it's great to be back in New Haven," the site of her graduate school alma mater, Yale, Harvard's chief rival. Still, she felt honored to be chosen in Cambridge. In being tapped for the Hasty Pudding honors, Meryl joined the ranks of Gertrude Lawrence, Katharine Hepburn, John Wayne, Elizabeth Taylor, Bob Hope, and Paul Newman. It was good company.

According to Meryl, her husband "maintains an amazing objectivity" about her success. If Gummer was in fact suffering from the "Mr. Streep" syndrome, Meryl didn't let anyone know. That was their problem, she thought, not something to be debated publicly. "It's demeaning to talk about something that means a lot," she says whenever the questions get sticky.

In January, she suffered the first of many traumas that afflict new parents. On the night the New York Film Critics planned to doubly honor her for *The Seduction of Joe Tynan* and *Kramer vs. Kramer*, Gippy became ill. After several frantic phone calls to her parents in Connecticut, her father drove to New York to pick up the award for her. He tried to allay Meryl's fears about the baby's condition. As the night progressed, Gippy's fever worsened. His forehead was burning, his cheeks were mottled red. Meryl and Gummer rushed their two-month-old infant to New York Hospital, the site of his birth. "It was just one of those high fevers that babies occasionally run," says a spokesman for the hospital. But the incident brought home the tenuous nature of new life. Her baby couldn't tell her what was wrong. Gippy's inability to communicate frightened the actress, who was reliant on every nuance of speech.

After the incident, she preferred not to leave her baby's side. Meryl's constant fear of losing control intensified when it came to Gippy's welfare. The dilemma heated up when Alan Alda called and asked her to join him in England for a promotional tour for *The Seduction of Joe Tynan*. Gummer, working on a new sculpture, was totally immersed in his work and wouldn't leave. The British round of interviews and public appearances with Alda would also keep Meryl busy. Guilt over Gippy was insidiously creeping into her thoughts. Grandma Streep provided a solution. She wouldn't baby-sit with the child in America, but if she could come along on the trip . . .

The two women and the infant left for England a few days later. Because Gippy had been so recently ill, they flew on a Concorde to lessen traveling time. From then on, Gippy's welfare would become top priority. The situation forced a decision on Meryl. She knew she would even be willing to give up her career for her family, because, she says, "No enterprise is bigger than your life's needs or your humanity."

Although Meryl had refused to hire a nurse at Gippy's birth, when she returned from her trip she hired a nanny "to help out one or two afternoons a week so that I can go out." The additional person in the loft crowded the young family.

New York begins to lose its glow without proper elbow room.

And raising a child in New York has its drawbacks. As Nikita Khrushchev noted on his first visit: "There is no greenery. It is enough to make a stone sad." Fresh air is in short supply. The flowers and trees that Khrushchev missed can be found on sometimes dangerous walks through Central Park, but there the natural wonders look more like caged animals, aberrations in a world of towering steel and glass. This is what Meryl the new mother was feeling after she returned from England. The lush green farmland near Godalming, in Surrey, remained a vivid memory. Meryl could still smell the damp loam and picture the weathered faces of farmers and their wives standing on the land they tilled themselves. The images became an escape valve for Meryl. Whenever the phone rang too often, or Gippy went stir-crazy in the small space, Meryl thought of Surrey, just a short trip from London. And then she took action. Meryl went house-hunting in the country.

Her needs were simple. She wanted a place within driving distance from Manhattan, but far enough away to see the stars at night.

The realtors had Georgian mansions and sprawling country estates in mind for America's hottest new actress. But in keeping with her relaxed style, Meryl chose a tiny, three-room cottage near Millerton, New York, for her second home. The house sits atop a mountain on ninety-two acres in Dutchess County, near the Connecticut border. She paid $140,000 for the property, which includes two other buildings. "We mortgaged ourselves for millions of years," Meryl says, a slight exaggeration for an actress who now commands one million dollars per picture.

"We bought a Christmas-tree farm with a fully furnished three-room house," she wrote to a friend in March 1980. "It's like having an apartment in the midst of a vast frontier, but it's part of our dream of becoming independent of the utility companies. We plan to install a windmill and a solar system. We also have five thousand Christmas trees," she continued. "It's wooded and quiet, and it's one of the precautions we're taking to safeguard our privacy."

When Meryl visits her upstate retreat, she rarely leaves the enclave of fir and pine trees that intoxicate her with a kind of pioneer spirit. In Millerton, she bubbles over with a sense of freedom, one that she is desperate to maintain. On weekends, she and Gummer like to eat out at an ultra-funky place called Billy's East Village. Diana Wu runs this converted gas station and serves a Chinese smorgasbord for twenty dollars a person. At André's health food shop in nearby Sharon, Meryl's often the first customer in the morning.

"It's cute," says a clerk there. "We all know who she is, but we don't let on. She comes in for vitamins or wheat germ, looks around, compares prices. She's wearing these gigantic purple sunglasses. It looks like she's pretending to be a movie star. Then she signs for her purchases. Not Meryl Streep. But Mary Louise Gummer."

When a small-town reporter breached a confidence and practically gave directions to Meryl's house in her article, the actress became livid. "I wrote her: 'What's going on in your mind? I don't live like the Kennedys. I don't have a compound and nine weimaraners running the grounds. You just make us sitting ducks.'"

Meryl is gravely troubled by the liabilities of stardom. After John Hinckley attempted to assassinate President Reagan in a deluded effort to endear himself to Jodie Foster, Meryl beefed up security at her Millerton retreat. She installed a sophisticated alarm system and even discussed hiring a guard. She lives with the constant worry that a lunatic will gain entrance and commit unspeakable acts. One eye is always directed over her shoulder.

Still, country living alleviates the other pressures of fame. It gives Meryl a chance to be herself. But often, when she tries to carry over her casual life-style to the world of Hollywood, the attempt backfires. Soon after she bought her cottage, she flew to Los Angeles for preliminary meetings about upcoming projects. She brought Gippy with her. At a lunch in the Polo Lounge of the Beverly Hills Hotel, the same place where she raised eyebrows when she swam in the pool, she sat and discussed the projects with her two-month-old baby strapped to her chest. The proffered scripts were simply not up to snuff.

"This is a particularly unadventurous time intellectually and artistically, even in terms of entertainment," she told her companions. "I feel worried, because my livelihood is threatened because I'm not interested in doing most of the films that are being made. People think you make choices based on some array of characters you've placed in front of you. Well, it isn't that way," she said. "There are so few beautifully written scripts that if there's something with any promise, you latch on to it. You pay to do it."

The dilemma is still a painful one for Meryl. But that day, nobody was really listening. They were trying to reconcile the image of this devoted mother with that of an important actress. "Very sixties-hippie reject," they said, after she left.

Every time the movie world fails to live up to her high expectations, Meryl spurns it like a girl with a back-up boyfriend. After the Hollywood meeting, she returned to New York with a re-ignited passion for the theater. Papp had finally agreed to resurrect *Alice in Concert*, the Elizabeth Swados project he had shelved a year earlier. The first time around, Meryl had invested all her psychic energy in the concert play and she wanted to stick with the project, no matter what its drawbacks were. Her agents advised that she back out, but she stood firm. She felt loyal toward the project and most especially toward its creator, Elizabeth Swados. The earlier reviews had singled out Meryl's talents while panning the show. It was a paradox she "felt guilty about," she says. How could a show be so lacking in quality, yet its star shine? This time Meryl believed all the components of *Alice* would be praised.

Nothing could have been further from the truth. Yet during rehearsals it seemed that Meryl herself might be *Alice*'s downfall.

She came down with the flu and refused to stop working. With laryngitis and a head cold, her naturally small voice disappeared. Papp was forced to postpone the show again. Meryl stayed in bed, guzzling orange juice and popping aspirins. But when the show opened a week later, Frank Rich of *The New York Times* wrote: "There is only one wonder in . . . *Alice in Concert*, and it goes by the name of Meryl Streep. Certainly it's more fun to sing Miss Streep's praises than contemplate Miss Swados' songs. Besides one leaves the Public [Theater] owing this star a considerable debt. Imagine Alice without her, and it's hard to picture any show at all."

Rich expressed shock that Meryl would involve herself with "the tuneless music," but praised her efforts. "At least Miss Streep, God bless her, insists on going on her merry way. Yet one must still wonder why she has devoted so much energy to this show, dating back to its original workshop presentation two years ago. Maybe, like Carroll's heroine, this actress took a drink from a mysterious bottle labeled 'Drink Me' and quite unwittingly, lost her head."

But Meryl wanted to lose her head, to become twenty different characters, spinning their yarns from voice to voice, from the White Queen to pigtailed Alice to Humpty Dumpty. Within five minutes onstage, ten at the most, Meryl willingly lost herself and became a host of other people in an exhausting, exhilarating feat of acting alchemy.

Milton Goldman and Sam Cohn, her agents at ICM,

were told to keep their feelers out for an unusual part. Like all good agents, they are merciless over the phone and sweet as saccharine in person.

"I've got to do something outside of Manhattan, outside of 1981, outside of my experiences," Meryl told them. "Put me on the moon," she said. "I want to be someplace else. I want to be held in the boundaries of a different time and place."

For once, her agents were speechless.

18

THE FRENCH LIEUTENANT'S WOMAN

A different century, a character so real that ambiguity defines her, a woman with a spirit strong enough to enslave others—that's the kind of part Meryl was after. And that's what she got.

The French Lieutenant's Woman was tailor-made to her request. John Fowles's painstaking re-creation of a passion thwarted by the strictures of Victorian England sold more than four million copies and was translated into eighteen languages. Sarah Woodruff, the once-responsible governess cast out of society for her shameless affair with an irresponsible sailor, was a part that many actresses craved. And, since the novel's publication in 1969, no fewer than five members of the movie elite wanted the property as their filmic tour de force.

With the part, Meryl would have to find the means to become an intense and mysterious woman, to give life to a strong but enigmatic character who rarely speaks.

And several directors wanted to join her on the project. Fred Zinnemann, the Oscar winner who had directed Meryl in *Julia*, had a script written by Dennis Potter, the British playwright. Mike Nichols wanted the property; so did Lindsay Anderson, Michael Cacoyannis, and Richard Lester. Author Fowles already had an actress in mind for the lead. He thought Vanessa Redgrave would make a perfect Miss Woodruff.

Fowles himself first approached Czech-born filmmaker Karel Reisz and asked him to direct the movie. Reisz had just finished *Isadora* and was reluctant to do another period piece. He turned it down.

But then he caught Meryl's performance as Kate in *The Taming of the Shrew* at the Public Theater. She mesmerized him. During her final speech, he knew he had met his Sarah Woodruff, his Tragedy, the woman in the long brown cape.

Instead of sounding like a tamed Kate in the play, Meryl justified the character's subservient words by infusing them with a love that demanded strength.

> Such duty as the subject owes the prince,
> Even such a woman oweth to her husband;
> And when she is forward, peevish, sullen, sour,
> And not obedient to his honest will,
> What is she but a foul contending rebel,
> And graceless traitor to her loving lord?

If she can do that with Shakespeare, Reisz thought, she will be able to instill dignity into Sarah Woodruff's abject desolation. He'd forgotten "she'd been with film for two and a half years," he said at the time. But after her performance as Kate, "I said to myself, 'Meryl's really flying now.' She had a range of temperament that is very rare and a special sort of daring." He knew then he would take on the project if it were still available.

Joseph Papp wasn't surprised at the influence Meryl had on Reisz. In *The Taming of the Shrew*, "Meryl took tremendous risks, both physical and emotional. I thought she was going to break every bone in her body when she threw herself on the floor playing Kate," he says. "There are only a few people I would call pure actors. Meryl is one. You can see it in her face. I've seen her cheeks get red, so that you can see the internal thing through her skin, which means there's a total emotional involvement in the situation."

Fowles was delighted at Reisz's change of heart, so delighted that he offered the director a free option on the property for a limited period of time. Then the difficulties set in.

"I admired the novel enormously from my first reading," Reisz says, "but I didn't see how to turn it into a drama. The novel had two exceptional qualities as a source for a movie: first, quite simply, it had a wonderful story centering on the extraordinary character of Sarah Woodruff—a turbulent, passionate spirit who is, so to speak, born into the wrong age. She has some of the visions of freedom we associate with the twentieth century, but was born, penniless, into the nineteenth.

"Secondly," he continued, "the novel was kind of a game: it told a Victorian story, but from the vantage point of today. Fowles continually invited us to view events with our modern knowledge; he played with the idea that he was only writing a fiction and shared some of his creative problems with us."

To be true to Fowles's conception, Reisz insisted it was impossible to tell the story without preserving the modern point of view. On the page, it was easy to perceive. All that was necessary was a change of tense: They did this, I say that. When Harold Pinter agreed to tackle the screenplay, he solved the problem by writing into the story a twentieth-century commentary to achieve the same effect visually. Sarah had to be literally transported into modern times. Pinter ended his screenplay with Sarah becoming a modern actress acting out her own life story on film and falling in love with her costar. "What with the two points of view in the novel," says Reisz, "it would have been cowardly not to have tried them both on film."

When Meryl read the screenplay, the unorthodox approach thrilled her. "I found it exquisite," she says. "Pinter's screenplay really hit the mark. When I read it, it elicited an emotional reaction in me and I determined to re-create it for someone else through thinking and design, thought and craft." After all, this was Pinter, the same genius she had studied in school. With *The French Lieutenant's Woman*, Meryl felt as if she was about to be initiated into the world of truly serious filmmaking.

But the technical aspects, however brilliant, were not all that sold Meryl on the screenplay. There was something else. Sarah Woodruff's obsession with her lost love was akin to Meryl's own reaction to Cazale's death. She had lived the life of this woman, jeeringly called Tragedy, for six painful months. In the movie, when Jeremy Irons tries to help her go on with her life and forget her lost love, she says, "For some things there is no comfort." They are the same words Meryl used when Cazale died.

It was a nervous time for Meryl. She worried that Fowles really wanted an English actress with big, dark eyes for the part. She worried that Reisz, a fatherly kind of director, resented the fact that she had appeared in *Holocaust*. He had lost his parents in the tragedy. Just before filming began, Meryl confided to an old college chum that she was "so frightened . . . frightened about something as important as this."

Still, she went ahead. For her largest role to date, she would be paid more money than she'd ever received: $350,000. That's not a large sum by Hollywood standards, but Meryl's strict attention to the artistic merits of a project prevented her from acting in what she deems "junk." The money pleased her because it would help the family. She could afford to hire a full-time nurse for Gippy and take the baby and her husband with her to England. For the first month, Gummer left his sculpting and joined his family.

Initially, she feared the wrath of her character's creator. She was petrified Fowles wouldn't approve of her playing the role. "Insofar as I had visualized Sarah, she wasn't really like Meryl," he says. "Sarah had these strange, rather large, exophthalmic eyes. And Meryl's face is more regular." Compounding her insecurities was Sarah's Victorian middle-class accent.

"Meryl was very concerned at first," Reisz recalls. "We even had it up our sleeve that we would lip-sync some of those parts if necessary."

She had never failed to meet a dramatic challenge before, and the idea of someone else's voice coming out of her screen presence sickened her. It was a John Gilbert tactic, a cheap trick perpetrated by silent screen stars who, somewhat like Nicholas and Alexandra, refused to give up their crowns when the sound revolution took place. If she couldn't find Sarah's voice within herself, Meryl thought she didn't deserve the part.

Twelve weeks before shooting commenced, she hired a vocal coach and spent long periods, sometimes three hours at a stretch, reading aloud from Jane Austen and George Eliot. Austen's *Persuasion* was set in a Dorset coastal town much like the area where the film would be shot. Meryl concentrated on its ethos. Slowly, she began to sound like Sarah to herself. Then, when a girlfriend she had known since childhood called and didn't recognize her voice, Meryl knew Victorian pose had subsumed her own personality. Schizophrenics were treated with lithium for the same kinds of symptoms. It scared Meryl. She had already disappeared into her character and, until the unnerving phone call, she wasn't even aware the transformation had taken place.

She had found the means to play Sarah Woodruff, but Meryl had not yet discovered her heart. The character still posed problems because, Meryl says, "The reasons for her actions were so vague. I knew only that she was ambitious. And because so much was covered up during Victorian times, I had to come on as though there was a fire inside, while remaining outwardly calm. I had, as the English say, to be careful about not going over the top."

She accomplished this, to the point where her casting seemed inevitable, by playing each monologue "like a dialogue with myself. What my eyes said was the truth, and what came out of my mouth wasn't."

The costumes helped. Anything to take her mind off the inexplicable. But the costumes also made clear the essence of Victorian sensibility. The clothing told the story of an elaborate cover-up. Voluminous folds of cotton and chamois, like shrouds; capelets that were little nooks of deceit: it was the garb of a private hide-and-seek game. And like Sarah Woodruff, Meryl concealed herself in the material, too.

At Vassar and Dartmouth, she had studied costume design and consequently took a keen interest in Sarah's outfits, the authentic laces and braids bought in antique shops in Camden Passage. Reisz remembers that "she was prodigiously well-informed on the subject."

Off-camera, the actress discovered the picturesque beauty of Lyme Regis, the sleepy little fishing village on England's southwest coast. It was Fowles's hometown, a place in which he has chosen to live "just for the sheer pleasure of leaving it occasionally and having the opportunity to return."

In preparation for the film, the townsfolk dolled up their streets, inadvertently ruining its charm. Fresh coats of paint on store fronts had to be sullied. Pink houses in the fishing village were whitewashed. The crew recobbled the sleek tar streets, removed the commercial banners heralding electronics stores, and politely asked the natives to park their motor cars elsewhere for the duration.

They agreed to all the requests except for the removal of

TV antennas. The land of the small box—their ticket to a world of sequins and manicured hands and scantily clad bleached blondes singing all the latest—was sacred territory. Production designer Assheton Gorton installed portable aerials to alleviate the problem. Meryl was astonished, and slightly dismayed. If this quaint town was so firmly entrenched in the twentieth century, she thought, would there be any market at all for the movie? Looking around at all the natural wonders, she felt like waking each resident to his divine good fortune in living in such a place.

The terrain is rough, especially the Undercliff, the six-mile, steep coastal forest cut by deep chasms and filled with towers of chalk and flint. Meryl took long afternoon walks, with Sarah Woodruff's trademark cape billowing around her shoulders, on the one path that was accessible. Sometimes she'd bring Gippy, other times she'd picnic with her husband, but usually she took her walks alone. It was her way of keeping in touch with Sarah, the woman who spent much of her time musing about lost love on the same stretch of desolate terrain.

At the dollhouse inn where the cast and crew stayed, she dropped her sad character's guise and became an exultant mother. She breast-fed Gippy and changed his diapers; the nanny had little to do. When Gummer was forced to return to Manhattan to catalog his sculptures for a show, "The phone bills were enormous. For five weeks in Lyme Regis, it came to $500," Meryl says. "He just felt so cut off."

Although Meryl was still "intimidated" by *The French Lieutenant's Woman*, the crew lessened her fears. Mostly English, they had no idea who Meryl was. But they figured she must be big. After all, she was the star. "They were so polite to me," she says, "because they were so British, you know?"

But Jeremy Irons at first was not so keen on his costar. He was daunted by Meryl's frightening, overbearing push towards perfectionism. "Whenever she suggested something," he says, "I at least tried it. If ever there was a possibility of confrontation, I tried it her way." To Irons, American actresses were a different breed altogether.

Initially, Meryl's devotion to her craft may have cowed him, but he came to respect her during an especially difficult scene. "When we shot the barn scene, where Meryl wakes up to me watching over her, it wasn't going well after many takes,' he recalls. "So she came over to me and physically shook me and said, 'It's hard, it's hard. You have to do it though, it's never easy.'" Irons paid his dues with deference.

But in Meryl's view, one coincidence made them soul mates for life. In 1975, Irons had played Petruchio in *The Taming of the Shrew*. When Meryl discovered they had acted in the same play, she felt each knew more about the other's soul than if they had been lovers. And they had not, Meryl wished to make emphatically clear, ever once lost themselves to lust.

Oh, but that's not what Irons said. In an interview he gave soon after the film was completed, he revealed that their lovemaking scenes were real. "In order to reach the right emotional pitch," Irons said about the famous scene where he ravishes her on a tousled Victorian bed, "Meryl and I had to experience emotionally almost what the characters were experiencing. So for the day we shot our love scene, Meryl and I had an affair. And when the cameras stopped, our affair stopped." Meryl immediately issued a curt reply stating that the love scene between "two good pals" was nothing but "playacting under the direction of Karel Reisz." She would take no chances with her marriage. She knew that Gummer was sensitive enough about her fame and fortune without adding intimations of cuckoldry to his problems.

From the moment the movie opened with that long impassioned look that Meryl bestows on Irons, she knew everyone would assume they were madly in love. It was the inevitable conclusion of her consummate performance. As

Time magazine raved: "An actress who can manage that adequately is a remarkable technician. One who can do it well is a rarity of the sort that comes along once or twice in a decade. What Charles sees when the cloaked woman turns toward him is an alarming, elemental Sarah who blows through the film like a sea storm, a Sarah who defines the role for all time. Her name is Meryl Streep."

But Meryl had one gnawing regret, the big bad demon that would haunt her again during *Sophie's Choice*. She didn't think she was pretty enough for the part. Despite the masterful makeup job, the wild tangled mass of auburn hair achieved with electric rollers and dye, she would never look as though she had stepped out of a Titian canvas and into Lyme Regis. That's the effect she wanted.

"Watching the film," she says, "I couldn't help wishing that I was more beautiful. There comes a point when you have to look the part, especially in the movies. In Victorian literature, passion, an illicit feeling, was always represented by darkness. I'm so fair that dark hair makes me look like some old fish, so I opted for auburn hair instead. I really wished I was the kind of actress who could have just stood there and said it all."

But cinematographer Freddie Francis, who filmed Meryl on a succession of difficult rainy days, saw a different image from her candid self-assessment. "Let me explain it this way," he says. "When I was first introduced to her, I saw a normal-looking girl. Once on the set, and I suspected as much, she became transformed through her performance. When I looked through the camera, something magical seemed to come back from her. She has that elusive 'presence' so few stars possess—and only the camera can see."

With the idolatrous critical acclaim also came some sniping. In an especially vituperative piece in the *Daily News*, movie critic Kathleen Carroll, who is usually kind, seemed to blame Meryl herself for the gushing press coverage. She poked fun at the candid photographs accompanying *Time* magazine's September 1981 cover story on Meryl. "They are even more ludicrous than the passionate prose," Miss Carroll stated. "In one artsy shot, Streep stares seductively at the camera from the window of her visibly ancient Tribeca loft. She then turns up surrounded by sullen-faced commuters on a graffiti-splattered subway car wearing not only an impossibly cheerful smile, but a demure, off-the-shoulder cotton dress. This, in the terrain of muggers and rapists.

"Streep, one is told, always travels by subway—except, apparently, on one occasion when this writer spotted her hailing a cab after what appeared to be a 5th Avenue shopping spree," she wrote.

Meryl was smart enough to realize her fall from grace would be a hard descent. But where was the parachute? What, no safety net? She was on her own. Meryl had never endeared herself to the press. They wanted a "scoop." What she gave them, time and again, was a short history of her intellectual development as an actress. In their eyes, she wasn't a star if she didn't live it up. Didn't she ever get drunk, silly, abrasive, abusive, they wondered? Where were the other men in her life? Why didn't she own a fur coat? Meryl is not, in the view of the ink-stained wretches, "good copy." So if she fell, they'd be merciless. She herself predicted that after the praise, it would be "time to dump the shit," and she braced herself for a pigsty's worth.

In March, producer Alexander Cohen tried to convince Meryl to be the hostess ("I hate that word," he says, "it conjures up someone with a menu") at the 1981 Tony Awards. She declined. She was afraid of becoming ubiquitous, an easy target for nasty pencils. She did agree to present one award, and in her nervousness forgot her speech.

The tides turned again. In June, Dartmouth College chose her to receive an honorary doctor of arts degree, despite the fact she'd criticized the school after spending part of her senior year of college there. Click, click, flash. The college photographer wouldn't let her alone. The school newspaper plastered her picture all over its front pages. Meryl became a memento. "You know, Ma, she's the one in the movies and she walked through my dorm." The mothers were pleased. "Such a nice girl. She finished college and now she's on TV."

The next month, she walked over to the 18th Street Playhouse to catch a high school friend, dark-haired, pretty Susan Castrilli, in three one-act plays by Tennessee Williams. Her brother-in-law Jack Gummer played the guitar for the performance. Onstage, they were giving their all. They basked in the overhead lights, the footlights, the exit signs. It was their time to shine. Against her will, Meryl ruined the evening. Everybody was watching her. The papparazzi caught her on camera in the lobby. She realized the press was an overbearing suitor.

She would not feel their true wrath until *Still of the Night* was released. She claimed the thriller, a takeoff on Hitchcock, would show "yet another Meryl Streep." The critics agreed. But this version was one they could do without.

19

THE BAD AND THE GOOD

For the first time since she became a star, Meryl chose a project she didn't really believe in, although *Still of the Night* was hard to resist for many reasons. It would reunite her with Robert Benton and Nestor Almendros, the writer-director and the cinematographer of *Kramer vs. Kramer*. Since it was shot around the chic haunts of the Upper East Side rich, Meryl could live at home with her beloved, and often neglected, family. She even secured a supporting role for her friend Joe Grifasi, who, as a detective in the film, wound up warning Roy Scheider about Meryl. She played a double murder suspect.

Meryl described her character "as a very, very rich person who works in an auction house. Roy is the psychiatrist who sort of loses his professional objectivity when he meets me." What he actually was supposed to do was fall in love with Meryl, the mistress suspected of murdering her lover, one of his former patients.

Newsweek magazine took out its rapier pen. "Scheider and Streep are no [Cary] Grant and [Grace] Kelly," wrote

David Ansen in his review. "You can't strike a flame with two metallic matches."

The main problem was a lack of rapport between Meryl and Scheider. Towards the end of filming, she admitted "there was a lot of tension" between them. It was partly the result of what they were asked to do in the script, based on a short story written by Benton and his one-time collaborator, David Newman.

Meryl's and Scheider's parts were tongue-in-cheek recreations of all the leading couples in classy movie mysteries ranging from Alfred Hitchcock's *Rear Window* to his *North by Northwest*. Meryl was not only cast as the typical blonde icicle, she also had to emulate predecessors such as Grace Kelly and Eva-Marie Saint—but in a role as artifical as polyester. And she couldn't do it. Meryl had no reference point.

"The dialogue seemed false," she says. "I got madder and madder because I knew the answer lay within me, but I couldn't wrestle it up. I sulked all day—something I never did before."

"She had to smoke a lot in the picture, as I recall," says Jessica Tandy, who played Scheider's mother, also a psychiatrist. "A chain-smoking neurotic. I think that added to the general feeling of nervousness."

The movie was set in the world of $100-an-hour shrinks, coats of endangered species, Chivas Regal, and lead crystal—to this day, a world in which Meryl has a hard time fitting in. Benton still had his intuitive confidence in her. Given a yellow legal pad and couple of sharp No. 2 pencils, she came up with an subplot involving her father, an American ambassador in Italy, whom her character was accused of pushing to death. "Working with Meryl," Benton says, "is like working with another writer. She's a wonderful collaborator. She's a combination of intelligence, imagination, and instinct.

"All right, I love her," he says. "Besides, we both like to garden."

But Meryl admits the movie was a mistake, that from the start she had a "who-the-hell-cares attitude" about the story.

"My flaw is that I did it because I love Benton and I wanted to work with him again. It was shot in New York, so I just rolled out of bed to go to work. I was with my baby more than I had ever been. I didn't have to work every day." This list trailed on.

"But listen," Meryl says, "I'm not ashamed of what I did, I just wished we'd all aimed higher." She makes an indirect reference to Benton: "People who are smart can't just do something that they think will be popular just because it's selling now. But you know what, *Still of the Night* will disappear. I have a certain confidence."

In that regard, her instincts were right.

Show business works like a drug. Sometimes it wears off, like the piddling mediocrity of *Still of the Night*. But the highs are blinding, giggle-inducing moments, like one Meryl shared with Benton a year earlier at the Academy Awards.

She wore a white, jacketed, piqué ensemble with black buttons that made her look like Annie coming from the orphanage to call on Daddy Warbucks. It was the latest in Mystic, Connecticut, where her mother lived. Mrs. Streep helped her daughter pick it out. She rushed to dress and barely brushed her hair, which hung limply in tangled clumps around her face.

But when her name was called to pick up the Best Supporting Actress award for *Kramer vs. Kramer* on April 14, 1980, all that anyone saw was her smile. It intensified her angles. "Holy mackerel!" she said when she picked up her first Academy Award and blinded the TV monitors with her cheekbones. "I can't hear what I'm saying 'cause my heart is beating so loud."

It turned out to be a ménage à cinque with a guy called Oscar: Meryl won, Dustin Hoffman won, and Benton's picture took three top awards. It was a New York kind of night for the Manhattan-based winners. At a small party afterwards, the guests discussed literature and art. No one was tasteless enough to bring up the losers, but Meryl had beaten quite a distinguished crew.

She had won her first Academy Award over Jane Alexander, who costarred with her in *Kramer vs. Kramer* as the neighbor who befriends Hoffman once Meryl leaves; Barbara Barrie, the suburban mother of the avid cyclist in *Breaking Away*; Candice Bergen, Burt Reynolds's flaky wife in *Starting Over*; and Mariel Hemingway, Woody Allen's teenage girl-friend in *Manhattan*, another movie in which Meryl had a part.

Her faithless lover, the press, tried to win back her favors. They descended on her like ants on a chicken leg. They blocked the exit from the Dorothy Chandler Pavillion. Meryl started to sweat.

But when she and Gummer managed to get out, she was not clutching her husband as she had done a year earlier when she'd lost for *The Deer Hunter*. This time she clutched Oscar. A lone reporter asked her how she felt. Meryl rubbed her forehead. Oscar was in her other arm—like a teddy bear, like a good luck talisman, like something she'd won for herself at a county fair's shooting gallery. "Incomparable," she told him.

20

SAD TIMES

When one is accustomed to success, when failure is only an intellectual concept, the pain of losing hurts more. Now that Meryl had begun to enjoy awards, like so many notches in a cowboy's belt, she fully expected to keep chalking up triumphs. All signs pointed toward another Oscar for *The French Lieutenant's Woman*. And this time, Meryl felt she actually deserved to win.

The preliminary contests were settled in her favor. On January 15, 1982, the Los Angeles film critics voted Meryl best actress. She flew out for the presentation and sat dreamy-eyed throughout it. She let the good vibes wash over her. There was, she decided, really nothing wrong with winning. The Puritan was becoming a hedonist.

In March, she received the same honor from England when the British Academy voted her best actress for *The French Lieutenant's Woman*. This time, she almost missed the presentation. Her acceptance speech was to be aired in England via satellite. She took the subway to the midtown studio for the taping. Midway through the ride, the train conked out. She hopped into a taxi. Michael Caine, who presented her with the award, remembers Meryl as "this harried young lady rushing into the studio, talking about traffic jams," just seconds before she appeared on the air.

The Academy Award was beginning to look more and more like a shoo-in. Before the ceremony, Meryl hosted a pre-win, family party at Mama Siltka's, a trendy, expensive omelette and seafood bistro near her Soho loft. She wore a red oriental jacket and black silk trousers. After wearing somber black and brown woolens and muslins in *The French Lieutenant's Woman*, Meryl had developed a taste for rich, colorful clothes. Her father and mother toasted her success, the happiness of her marriage, their new grandson. Meryl forgot Gippy was at home with a nanny and requested a high chair at the table. "A half hour later," a waiter recalls, "she asked me to take it away. Her son wasn't coming. But she seemed to miss him so much that the empty high chair upset her." The constant push and pull between family duties and career obligations were making Meryl edgy.

Then Katharine Hepburn won the Oscar for *On Golden Pond*, and Meryl was devastated.

United Artists made matters worse. The studio decided to advertise *The French Lieutenant's Woman* with the line, "She loved only one man, but they called her the French Lieutenant's Whore." Meryl fumed. She felt the campaign was a cheap shot. Not only was the phrase purposely misleading, it debased the relationship she had worked so hard to achieve on the screen. And it was something she wouldn't want bombarding the eyes and ears of her family in print campaigns, radio advertisements, and TV commercials. As always, Meryl was protective of her inner circle. She wanted to shield them in the same way she wanted to preserve her own privacy.

But she was back in the limelight that year to accept more accolades. She picked up an Obie award for her performance in *Alice in Concert*. And there was a string of lunches and dinners with agents, reporters, producers—even Sherry Lansing, then president of Twentieth Century–Fox and the first woman to head a studio, wined and dined Meryl.

Night life was taking its toll on Gummer, though. At the opening party for Arthur Penn's movie *Four Friends* at the Russian Tea Room, he showed up wearing an old pea coat and sipped a vodka quietly in a corner while Meryl congratulated Jodi Thelan, the movie's star. She chatted with Penn and Steve Tesich, the screenwriter. Gummer just ate his chicken Kiev and blinis. He didn't know these people. And their specialized vocabulary—options, turnarounds, development deals, long shots, short takes—left him speechless. The talk was out of his realm; it bored him. With a false air of patience, he smiled for the cameras when photographers snapped him and Meryl with Reed Birney and Natalia Nogulich, other players in the movie.

The Gummers went to the Broadway opening of Beth Henley's Tony Award–winning *Crimes of the Heart* to applaud Meryl's dear friend Mary Beth Hurt. There was quite a scene at the John Golden Theater—Cyndy Garvey and Marvin Hamlisch arrived arm in arm, adding fuel to the rumors of their romance. By comparison, Meryl and Gummer looked like an ordinary suburban couple. She wore a simple black peasant dress and Gummer came, tieless, in old corduroy pants and a tweed jacket stained with white paint. At the Winter Garden, however, they received as much attention as Jackie Onassis when they showed up at the dance premiere of Twyla Tharp's *Catherine Wheel*, but Gummer convinced Meryl to skip the party afterwards at Studio 54.

During the daytime, Meryl was temporarily caught up in a whirlwind of social occasions. There was a luncheon she had to attend at the Warwick Hotel in honor of *The French Lieutenant's Woman*. Then New York's Governor Hugh Carey invited the best and brightest (read: most visible) actors from the metropolitan area for a party at Tavern on the

Green. And Meryl, who loves New York things like the subway and egg creams and bagels and Sicilian pizza, felt it was her civic duty to attend.

The governor, however, couldn't make it to his own party. It had been a well-orchestrated publicity stunt on his part to push the virtues of filming in New York. But a lot of his acting constituents showed up. Roy Scheider came in jeans. Polly Bergen and Anne Meara giggled at the comic antics of Anne's husband, Jerry Stiller. Joan Fontaine, Christopher Plummer, Maureen Stapleton, and Piper Laurie made appearances. Barbara Barrie brought her kids.

The greenhouse room, the most desirable banquet hall in the establishment, was full of stars. Waiters offered trays of goat-cheese puffs, steak tartare, and miniature quiches. Flickering white lights on the trees outside the room added a festive air. Central Park, visible through the windows, looked safe and green and inviting.

Patti LuPone, William Hurt, Sigourney Weaver, and Bob Balaban stood talking together like the young guard of the screen. Meryl chatted with Melvyn Douglas, hugged Justin Henry, and then she and Al Pacino talked about John Cazale. He gladly reminisced about her late lover, sharing his stories of being on the set with "so talented an actor." Talking about Cazale brought back painful memories. Shortly thereafter, a limousine whisked her home.

21

SOPHIE'S CHOICE

When Meryl began reading a novel by William Styron called *Sophie's Choice*, the power of his lyrical descriptions of Sophie Zawistowska took her mind off everything else. She pored over the 515-page hardcover edition of the novel; she reread it so many times that sections of it were committed to her memory. She knew then she wanted the role of Sophie more than she'd ever wanted anything. "I really, desperately, wanted that part," she says.

The novel is vaguely autobiographical. Styron, like his protagonist Stingo, was once a young Southern writer who loved Thomas Wolfe so much he moved to Brooklyn, where he lived in a boarding house much like the Pink Palace of the movie. Once there, the author really did meet a Sophie—one Sophie Bieganski. "She told me she had been at Auschwitz. Nothing much more," he says. "She had a tattoo. And a huge yearning to eat." Years later, Styron had a dream about her—a mandate, he called it—and he stopped working on a novel about the Marines and began work on *Sophie's Choice*. The possibility of making it into a movie thrilled him.

At the other end of the film project was multimillionaire

132

Florida land developer Keith Barish. As his first venture in movie producing, in May 1979 he bought the Styron novel for Alan J. Pakula to direct. Barish paid $750,000 for the property. Almost immediately, he recalls with relish, "I was getting bites from studios and production companies to back the movie." By July, he decided on Sir Lew Grade's Marble Arch productions, headed by Martin Starger. They agreed to make the book into a twelve-million-dollar movie. Everything was going as smooth and fast as a slalom race on new snow. Then they hit an obstacle. Negotiations came to a standstill whenever casting was discussed.

Styron says he always "pictured Ursula Andress as Sophie: a wild lioness, a tangled mane of emotion." Meryl admits she called Pakula and "begged him for the part." But Pakula strongly insisted that three unknowns play the main parts of Stingo, Nathan, and Sophie. Then he toyed with the idea of a relatively unknown actor—perhaps Philip Anglim—in the role of Stingo. Starger convinced Pakula that at least one big star would be necessary for box-office appeal and that the natural star role was Nathan's.

Pakula began pondering the male possibilities. All of them were "right, but a little wrong," he says. He became obsessed with finding the right Nathan. At home with his wife, Hannah, in the middle of telling a funny anecdote he'd break off in mid-sentence, begin to stare, and think about actors. He thought Al Pacino, closest physically to Styron's Nathan, was "the rightest," but he lacked "bourgeois Jewishness." Dustin Hoffman, according to the director, "had Nathan's wild inventive sense," but not his "sadomasochistic romantic quality that makes people of both sexes fall in love with him." And Robert De Niro possessed "the charismatic quality, but not the humor." Pakula was afraid to make one false step with the book he so loved.

The actors were on his mind, but the actresses were the ones who began contacting Pakula. In addition to Meryl, a battery of talented, beautiful actresses began phoning about Sophie's part. But Pakula already had someone in mind for the pivotal role: Liv Ullmann.

"She was ten years older than Sophie, who's twenty-eight for most of the book," says Pakula. "But I thought she could play the harsh realities and ambivalences. And she was a woman with whom a young boy would fall in love." More importantly, she possessed the "foreignness" Pakula deemed essential for the part. "If I hadn't decided to write the screenplay myself, she would have had the role," Pakula says.

The reason was that writing took longer than he anticipated and shooting had to be postponed for two years. In the interim, Marthe Keller rang him up and told the director the book had changed her life. She would do anything for the part. Barbra Streisand wanted it, too. She was so enthusiastic she was willing to play Sophie without a salary—just percentage points in the movie. Pakula couldn't imagine Sophie being so pragmatic about business. Thankfully, Sir Lew Grade didn't think Streisand looked the part.

Then director Andrzej Wajda called Pakula. He thought Meryl Streep would be ideal. It was quite a compliment for Meryl, coming as it did from a Polish national. But Pakula wasn't convinced. He had emissaries in Europe searching for an unknown.

And then he found her. Her name was Magda Vasaryova.

A few months later, nobody could even remember what she looked like. Poetic license had influenced their casting decision. It was her name, the heavy-sounding Magda, that enthralled them. But her English was poor. She'd have trouble getting a visa. Pakula began to mull over Wajda's recommendation. "Meryl Streep seemed a woman of great strength, great intelligence, great craft," he says. "She came across to me as a very admirable young American woman.

But that had little to do with Sophie. Nothing I had ever seen Meryl in made me think she could play Sophie."

Eventually he began to change his mind. "Then there were only two people in the world I could see in the part," Pakula says. "Magda and Meryl."

Meryl visited him at his office. "I told her there were three things I was concerned about. One was foreignness. Another was that kind of raw sensuality. And the third was strength." These were no minor quibbles. The movie's success rested on them.

"The tragedy of Sophie," Pakula told Meryl, "is her vulnerability, and the fact that she feels she is totally lacking in heroic qualities in this time that seems to demand an almost impossible heroism—a time which beyond forcing monstrosities on the victim, forces guilt as well." His fear was that Meryl as Sophie would turn out "as Joan of Arc," he says. "Then the film would be in trouble."

But he offered Meryl a screen test anyway. For an actress of her renown, the idea of a test was almost a slap in the face. She swallowed her pride and said she would take it. But it never took place.

Meryl went off to film *The French Lieutenant's Woman*; Pakula stayed in America and made *Rollover*. Months later, out of the blue, he offered her the part. Meryl tempered her initial enthusiasm. She demanded to see a completed script first. The request startled Pakula. He began to reconsider Magda.

The intrigue grew. Meryl obtained a pirated copy of the script "through nefarious means," she says. Her agents had probably secured it. But the script hooked her. "I went to Pakula and threw myself on the ground. 'Please God, let me do it,' I begged."

Pakula remembers her "passion. I went home, slept on

it, woke up and thought: She has the kind of passion I had when I read the book." But he made no decision.

To get his mind off casting, Pakula went to Central Park and saw *The Pirates of Penzance* with Kevin Kline. "There's a very good chance this man can play Nathan in *Sophie's Choice*," he told friends. Kline was flabbergasted.

"I never believed I would end up playing Nathan," he says. "When the novel was first published in 1979, a friend of mine said to me, 'I just read a fantastic book which is going to make a great movie. There's a part in it that would be perfect for you, but they'll probably get some movie star to play it.'" Meryl is partially responsible for his being chosen. On the day Pakula told her that he was still considering Magda and would make a decision in ten days, she put in her own plug for Kline. "O.K.," Meryl said. "But whether I play the role or not, I'll tell you who would make a wonderful Nathan—Kevin Kline."

The coincidence was too great to ignore. Pakula met with Meryl once more. "I don't know what you're going to do with the role," he told her, "but I'll take the chance."

Meryl began learning Polish and German. She studied five days a week for three months. "I don't know how I see my character yet," she said during the first week of her language lessons. "I'm still in the 'intuit' stage, and I haven't picked her apart yet. First I'll learn Polish. Then I'll forget me. Then I'll get to her. That's my plan of action."

It was similar to her preparation for *The French Lieutenant's Woman*—slow, studious, almost plodding. She hoped that during these preliminary stages, she'd be graced again with the soul of her character. Meryl, and the whole movie-going public, would not be disappointed. Even as understandably fussy a critic as Styron, the author whose words gave the character life, sings Meryl's praises. "Her performance is simply the most amazing that I've ever seen," he says.

The first day of shooting took place at the Gould Memorial Library of Bronx Community College. As circumstances turned out, it was also the scene where Sophie and Nathan first meet. Pakula's desire to shoot in sequence as often as possible was "a perfect way of working," Kline recalls. "We got to know one another on screen in the natural order. That enabled us to grow on camera." In fact, he and Meryl were so grateful to Pakula they arranged for a string trio to surprise him during a lunch break. Champagne flowed. "To Sophie," Meryl toasted. "To a difficult, important movie."

The story of Stingo's 1947 summer friendship with the bewitching, secretive Sophie and her brilliant, troubled boyfriend, Nathan, was told in a series of flashbacks in the book. Pakula decided to stick with the conceit, however difficult it would be to film. He cast Peter MacNicol as Stingo.

In March 1982, interior sets were built in Manhattan's Camera Mart studios. Production was finished a startling three months later in Zagreb, Yugoslavia, at the Jadran Studios. It was there that the Auschwitz scenes of unforgiving bleakness were shot.

In New York, the Brooklyn Bridge became a backdrop for parts of the American shoot. The ramshackle, homey boarding house in the movie, the Pink Palace, was actually a dove-gray Victorian mansion on Brooklyn's renovated Rugby Road. Owner Phil Toia rented it to the movie crew for about $1,000 a day. They painted it eyesore pink, with the promise of repainting after a week's worth of shooting. During the exterior shots, Toia said his mother-in-law was so impressed with Meryl Streep she came over during the evening shooting and stayed up all night.

Problems came in the second month of production. The Polish language stumped Meryl. "I was good in languages, French and Italian, in school, and I thought 'Well, I'll just pick it up right away.' But it was tough," she says.

By the time filming began, she could "understand Polish, but I couldn't speak it that well. It's a tough language, because you have to parse the sentence as you speak it—the objects and modifiers change their endings, depending on where they are in the sentence."

"But she did it with artistic exactitude. I never knew she had a problem," Styron says. "I've known many Polish women and I was astounded by her flawless accent."

It also astounded her family, at the same time distressing them. While filming the scenes in Brooklyn, she'd rush home every night to cook dinner. She'd make chicken cutlets, veal, something simple after her long day, anything to be alone with Gummer and Gippy. But the baby didn't recognize her voice. She'd bend over to comfort him and he'd burst into tears. She wasn't mimicking an accent in *Sophie's Choice*. She had searched for the gutteral sounds within herself and once she found them, she couldn't drop them at will. "I used to think how hard it must have been for her," Pakula says. "It upset the baby. It really frightened him."

Pakula found her dedication to work and home a little overwhelming. "As a man, I don't know how that's done," he admits. "Creative gifts, I think, are tougher for a woman than a man. To make all that work—playing Sophie, the emotional explosions, the terrors of that extraordinary role—and then to go home to her husband and son and make dinner!"

But in a way, he was envious. "It gave her a sense of reality and stability through the shooting. Many lesser talents with whom I've worked are more precious about their gifts. Meryl refuses the protection of cotton batting. She wants to do her own shopping at the grocery. She wants to know how much things cost. She doesn't want to lose touch with the real world," he says.

And the everyday, ordinary ups and downs are tantamount to her continued success. "It seems to me," she says, "that when you become famous, a lot of your energy goes into maintaining what you had before you were famous, maintaining your sense of observation, being able to look at other people. If they take away your observation powers, you're lost."

Considering the difficult circumstances under which the movie was made, Meryl's achievement in *Sophie's Choice* is all the more stunning. She was hounded by the press while filming the Brooklyn scenes. When Poland refused to allow entry to the film crew, Pakula hastily made arrangements for the cast and technicians to shoot in Yugoslavia. Meryl had to leave her family for an extended period of time. She had to gain ten pounds for the Brooklyn scenes, and then lose twenty-five for the concentration camp scenes. And she had to shave her head.

But all the sacrifices were worth it, in Meryl's view, because Sophie "had some humor. She was funny. On the screen, I hadn't been able to play that before."

It wasn't until long after casting that Pakula was convinced Meryl would be able to pull off the role. "I only saw Sophie [in her] the first day of reading, when Meryl opened her mouth, and suddenly the character came out."

She took the real Sophie's appetite and transformed that hunger into a rapaciousness for life's present moment, for good times, for an end to horrific memories. When she curled her hair and put on the flowered chemises, the ratty ostrich boas, the amber beads, the red nail polish, the felt plumed hats, she became the jaunty Polish immigrant beating back the imminence of death. She became for Styron the culmination of his prose. She gave his ideas life.

By then Pakula, too, was hooked. Later, in Yugoslavia, he gave up trying to direct her. "I would never push Meryl in any direction of my own until I saw the direction she chose to take," he admits. "Often, it was not what mine would have been; but it had more authenticity, more originality."

Awe is a hard thing to hide. Meryl knew, in her own way, that she had them all in her back pocket. Pakula and the rest, including cinematographer Nestor Almendros and actor Josef Sommer, who'd both worked with Meryl on *Still of the Night*, couldn't disguise their amazement at her uncanny ability to become Sophie. But familiar duties were preventing her from going all the way.

On the weekend before the harrowing concentration camp scenes were about to begin shooting, Meryl wanted to leave Yugoslavia. She asked for some time off. Gummer was opening his one-man show at the Spirone Westwater Fisher Gallery in New York. Meryl left Pakula a note in the makeshift production office: "I don't know how you're going to feel about this, but please consider it anyhow." She proposed to fly to New York on Saturday, turn up at the Soho art gallery on Sunday, and on the same day, take the first available flight back to Yugoslavia. "I'll be there in time for work on Monday morning," she promised. "Don's always there for me," she told Pakula. "I'm eating myself up that I can't be there for him."

Pakula had always distrusted planes. What if something happened? Besides, even if all went smoothly, he thought Meryl would be exhausted by the ten-hour journey.

A crew member recalls his predicament. "I wouldn't want this known, but I advised Alan to say no. He asked me what I thought. I thought it was a play for sympathy, a girly-girl wanting attention."

Pakula decided to risk it. "I trusted her totally," he says. "I had to. And I knew that not being there would really eat her up."

She flew home and was able to be with her husband for an afternoon. On Monday morning, she was back in Yugoslavia, early for the shoot, and "her work was terrific," Pakula recalls with amazement.

Meryl is frankly thrilled by her performance as Sophie,

but she credits the role more than her interpretation. "Has there been a character that interesting in the movies in a long time?" she asks. "There are so many choices throughout the film—whether she should live with Stingo or die with Nathan, whether she should kill herself in church or live with the guilt of refugees. But what is great about her is that she does make the choices, but then, if she has made the wrong one, she doesn't quit: She goes on till the next thing hits her."

As for the wrenching climax, "there's no speck of reasoning in that moment," Meryl says about Sophie's decision to die. "And as an actress, I can't tell you why she does what she does. You can't plan how you're going to act in an emergency. There is no logic, and that's the point."

She defused critics, including Holocaust survivor and author Elie Wiesel, who believed the depiction of the horrors of Nazi Germany trivialized the truth. "I do worry about that happening," Meryl says, "but I don't think I've contributed to it. On the other hand, people are never really going to be moved by a big statistic. You have to try to reach them with the horror through the heart."

In fact, the movie so thrilled her, she hated to finish it. "The only real thing tough about the part was saying goodbye to it," she says. "I could have played it forever. It was wonderful, the best thing I've ever experienced."

Critics agreed and applauded her performance as the best of the year. "The truth is that *Sophie's Choice* is a one-woman show," wrote Meryl's erstwhile critic, Kathleen Carroll of the *Daily News*. "Miss Streep accomplishes the near impossible, presenting Sophie in believably human terms without losing the scale of Mr. Styron's invention. In a role affording every opportunity for overstatement, she offers a performance of such measured intensity that the results are by turns exhilarating and heartbreaking. Thanks in large to

Miss Streep's bravura performance, it's a film that casts a powerful uninterrupted spell."

Rex Reed of the *New York Post* admitted that the movie caused him to change his mind about Meryl. "Before I saw *Sophie's Choice*," Reed said, "the alleged magic of Meryl Streep eluded me totally. I didn't understand what the fuss was about.

"At best," he continued, "she seemed like a gifted, well-trained professional victimized by bad habits and irritating mannerisms. At worst, she seemed like a frozen, boring blonde with ice water in her veins, from the Grace Kelly–Tippi Hedren School of Dramatic Art. I simply didn't get the message.

"Now I do. As Sophie Zawistowska, the beautiful, tragic Polish immigrant who survived Auschwitz to be tortured by her memories in post-war Brooklyn, she is positively mesmerizing."

He couldn't contain himself in his review. The *New York Post*, which prides itself on short, pithy articles, was forced to jump his piece on *Sophie's Choice* to a second page. "Butchering the English language, struggling to forget the past, trying to pull the jagged shards of her life together, her work is so natural and full of unexpected insights that she makes each scene a marvelous adventure.

"It's hard enough for an all-American girl from New Jersey to play an ill-fated Blanche DuBois with the demons of World War II written all over her, but Streep does it in not one but three separate languages. She gives the performance of the year, and I am happy to eat crow. Not often—but sometimes—a critic is the last to know," Reed wrote.

But the praise upset Meryl a little. "Nothing can match all this build-up," she says. "I mean, it's a movie. You go to see it, you sit there, and that's it." What she failed to say was that for most moviegoers, her haunting portrayal of Sophie would be etched indelibly on their brains. With that one performance, Meryl moved up the ranks from consummate actress to screen legend.

22

NO MORE NUKES

On June 12, 1982, Central Park became a sea of worried faces banded together in protest against nuclear proliferation. And Meryl clasped hands with her fellow protestors.

In previous months, she had avoided speaking out on the emotion-fraught issue because she was fearful of being crucified by reporters, whom she thought would "invariably make some crack about Jane Fonda," she says. But then she didn't care. She felt too strongly about the issue to worry about appearances any longer. So she became a visible opponent of the arms race and marched along with one million other people.

"We've got to do everything we can to make ourselves felt, and not just talk about the nuclear threat," she says. "We've got to write our congressmen and read books like Jonathan Schell's *The Fate of the Earth*. We can't withdraw into a deadening end-of-the-world fear, so deep-rooted that we don't even recognize it in ourselves."

She helped organize a benefit at the Beacon Theater and then convinced Richard Dreyfuss, James Earl Jones, Jill

Clayburgh, Arthur Miller, and Colleen Dewhurst to perform with her on June 7, 1982. The star-studded cast helped draw an equally celebrated audience. Robert De Niro, Judd Hirsch, Jack Weston, Constance Cummings, Alexander Cohen and his wife Hildy Parks, Jack Gilford, Ellen Burstyn, Julie Belafonte, Sheldon Harnick, and Bob Balaban all arrived to lend support.

Mothering a child intensified her desire for nuclear disarmament. "I keep thinking all the time that, in the year 2000, Gippy will be only twenty-one," she says. "I've found that as my responsibilities multiply, so does my own stake in the future of the world."

In December, poet Rose Bergunder, a founding member of Amnesty International and wife of William Styron, organized the premiere screening of *Sophie's Choice* as a benefit for the worldwide human-rights organization. In addition to the cast, the gala event drew Dick Cavett, Geraldine Stutz (owner of Henri Bendel), writers Frank Perry and Barbara Goldsmith, composers Adolph Green and Betty Comden, Phyllis Newman, and Beatrice Straight. But nobody recognized Meryl. She was bone thin, with her real brown hair cut in a short shag haircut in preparation for *Silkwood*, a movie in keeping with her new political activism. Its director, Mike Nichols, inadvertently started a real war with another project.

There was only one woman who could best Meryl Streep at the point after *Sophie's Choice* opened. The one actress whose grip on the imagination of the American public was stronger at that time—and always had been and always would be—won a fierce battle against Meryl. Her name? Elizabeth Taylor.

Through their agents and producers, the two women engaged in a behind-the-scenes fight for the rights to *Private Lives*, the Noel Coward comedy about divorced lovers. It was like Queen Elizabeth arguing with Queen Mary. Zev Bufman, who had been romantically linked to Miss Taylor when she brought *The Little Foxes* to Broadway, said that he narrowly beat Mike Nichols for *Private Lives*. "Mike wanted to do it himself, directing and costarring with Meryl Streep," says Bufman. "But I got the Noel Coward estate to work with us instead. I asked Mike to direct it for us, but he said his schedule wouldn't permit it." Presumably, he wouldn't think of doing the play without Meryl either.

Instead, Nichols cast her in *Silkwood*, his controversy-ridden screen biography of Karen Silkwood, the twenty-eight-year-old laboratory technician who died in a mysterious car crash after being radioactively contaminated. Her unsolved death in 1974 has been linked to attempts to silence her for speaking out about the dangers of nuclear energy.

"It's the kind of character I haven't done before," says Meryl. "She's a small-town Texas girl who has been displaced to an Oklahoma factory to produce fuel rods for a nuclear plant. Someone who is close to being me." Somehow, the similarities are not immediately apparent.

Meryl explains: "She is a lot like me, my real personal self. She has a lot of humor, is a little sassy, gets a lot of people mad at her, and she does what she believes she has to do."

Cher, who plays her best friend in the movie, admits she was "frightened of meeting Meryl. I thought it was going to be like having an audience with the Pope," she says. "Somebody so big she's out of this world. I mean, me and Meryl Streep?" she asks. "Never."

But they became good friends right away. "Meryl never tried to make me feel I wasn't up to par. After nineteen years in the business, this was the first time I felt people taking me seriously," Cher reveals. "She gave me pointers on acting, I advised her on singing."

While shooting in Texas, screenwriters Nora Ephron and Alice Arlen often joined Meryl and Cher during breaks.

"It was like Virginia Graham's 'Girl Talk,'" Cher admits.
"We'd knit, crochet, joke about men. And Meryl and I talked
about our kids so much I thought something was wrong with
us, that we didn't have an existence outside of them. Then I
realized we were just two proud mothers."

The movie caused so much of a stir before it was released that the Kerr-McGee Corporation, which owns the
nuclear plant where Karen Silkwood worked, considered
bringing a lawsuit against the producers to prevent its red,
white, and blue logo from being used in the picture.

Kurt Russell, the former baseball player who portrayed
Meryl's boyfriend in the movie, found the treatment of the
subject matter "almost totally opposed to my personal
views." Working with Meryl, however, was "one of the high-
lights of my career. She gives so much in a scene that it's
hard to keep up with her."

A month before *Silkwood* was released, Meryl and Nichols sneaked into a celebrity-studded screening at Loew's
Tower East in Manhattan. Meryl was worried. Fearing that
moviegoers might view the film as a treatise against nuclear
power, she wondered if they'd also view *Silkwood* as entertainment. "I'm not sure people are going to want to see this
movie," she said. "They may stay away from something that
smells like a message."

At the advance screening, she and Nichols hid in the
projection room and waited for Dustin Hoffman, Susan
Sarandon, Paul Simon, Woody Allen, Jeremy Irons, Richard
Widmark, Steve Martin, and the rest of the audience to be
seated before they quietly slipped into the last row of the
theater to gauge the audience reaction.

Meryl was happily surprised when the crowd cheered.
Her pleasure at *Silkwood*'s reception increased in direct pro-
portion to its long run.

When the movie officially opened on December 14,
1983, audiences had trouble connecting the gum-chewing,

coarse-voiced character of Karen Silkwood with the Meryl Streep they knew. But is is a testament to her acting ability that Meryl was able to persuade them to identify with Silkwood: a chain-smoking, beer-drinking redneck; a somewhat promiscuous divorced woman whose children live with their father. Her life seems to empitomize the frustrations of the ordinary working stiff. But she redeems herself, managing to rise to the occasion—even rise above it—when her situation becomes extraordinary.

"Everybody has a different idea who Silkwood was. A lot of special-interest groups have painted her as a savior, a martyr, a woman with a halo around her head," Meryl says. "But from what I could discover, her slate wasn't completely clean—like all of us; I got the feeling even more so with her. I was intrigued by the possibilities of that—the idea that people who do good things can be unsavory, that heroic acts can be performed by someone who doesn't immediately grab your heartfelt sympathy. I looked for clues to her motivation, and I tried to be truthful to the information we had, but it was tough: I realize that, in the end, my Karen Silkwood is different from what she was really like."

Karen Silkwood's own parents were dismayed by the movie, and especially Meryl's portrayal of their daughter. Karen was "a whole lot smarter than they showed in the movie," said Silkwood's father, Bill. Her mother, Merle, wondered why "those women from New York didn't ever call to ask about Karen. Why didn't they call Karen's father or any of Karen's teachers or freinds down here in Nederland?"

Yet Meryl's unstudied characterization-by-hunch helped the film transcend its initial image as antinuclear propaganda. Thanks to her performance *Silkwood* gained acceptance as a mainstream movie; in its first month of release it also made as much as it cost, twelve million dollars. The movie's hefty box-office gross was helped in part by the January 11, 1984,

U.S. Supreme Court decision to reinstate the ten-million-dollar award against Silkwood's employer, the Kerr-McGee Corporation.

When it came right down to it, Meryl paid more attention to Karen Silkwood's personality than to politics in her interpretation. The scene in which she flashes a breast to shock her factory coworkers "was very awkward for me," Meryl admits, "because I'm always so sensitive about women doing nude scenes. It's a personal gripe. I did it because, in context, I thought she probably would do something like that. It made sense. But it's still a completely bizarre and horrible thing to do in front of a crew."

Cher, on the other hand, was more affected by the issues in the movie. She says she broke down toward the end of the film "and had to get up and leave because I was almost hysterical" during the scene in which the doctors tell Silkwood she's not badly contaminated by plutonium. "I knew the doctors were lying," says Cher. "And Meryl was made up to look as if she was going to die. Suddenly I looked at her and thought: 'This happened to a real person.' And if Meryl were dying, I don't think I could stand it."

The political ramifications ran deeper for Meryl as a private citizen. She is most proud of the fact that the movie "seems to be accurate about people who have jobs, real people. It really made me think about life in a small town where there's one industry—how easy it is for me to say, 'Let's close that down,' but how people are worrying about their jobs and their kids and just hoping for the best, even in their boss; that if there were something dangerous, the company would fix it. So in fact, it gave me a better understanding of another side of the story.

"I've been a movie star for a while now, so I'm living in the stratosphere, but I remember well enough working in restaurants and similar jobs, and I understand how it's easy to think just about your own existence, just worry and work from paycheck to paycheck."

In her own life, Meryl was experiencing a similar fragmented existence, but on a much larger scale.

After *Silkwood* was completed, she went to Paris to dub the French version of *Sophie's Choice*. Gallic superstars Philippe Noiret and Isabelle Huppert dined with her at unpretentious Paris bistros where, over red wine, they became friends. Meryl is the kind of serious American actress the French adore. After farewells and a promise to mail them some books, Meryl took off for England to conduct a symposium on film. She realized she was exhausted. She cut short her stay and arranged for a family vacation. Meryl, Gummer, and Gippy arrived in Spain, where they lay on the beaches near the Costa del Sol, ate fish with green sauce, and avoided movie houses with a passion. They were an ordinary family out to have a magnificently normal good time.

They traveled together again for the 1983 Academy Awards, but this time the family did not go unnoticed. On her flight out, the stewardesses chuckled over the in-flight movie. The *Sophie's Choice* nominee would have to watch *An Officer and a Gentleman*, starring another contender for that year's best-actress award—Debra Winger, the working-class girl in love with officer Richard Gere. Meryl, the stewardesses said, "seemed to enjoy the movie."

Besides Miss Winger, Meryl was pitted against Julie Andrews as the cross-dresser in *Victor/Victoria*, Jessica Lange as the tormented actress Frances Farmer in *Frances*, and Sissy Spacek as the young widow in *Missing*.

"When I was going to California," Meryl recalls. "my dad called and said, 'If you win [for *Sophie's Choice*], when you get up there, keep it short, sparkling, and nonpolitical.' I told him my dress would sparkle enough for both of us, and if I could get up at all that moment I promised I wouldn't say one word about the [she makes a bomb noise]. That's a nice-sized audience, 300 million people, and the desire to say whatever you want to say to everybody on earth in two minutes is strong."

However, she took her father's advice because "I could see his point about what was appropriate at the moment," Meryl says. And when the envelope was opened and her name was called, all she could muster for the even larger audience, 500 million people around the world, was: "Oh boy." She dropped her speech, but she was beaming. "No matter how much you try to imagine what this is like, it's just so incredibly thrilling right down to your toes."

Her pleasure came primarily because her Oscar was for Sophie, her favorite part. But the string of statistics that went with the win were pretty impressive. If she were a baseball card, she'd have been dog-eared by the end of the evening. In fact, sequins were dropping from her gold and silver gown.

It was Meryl's fourth nomination and second Oscar win in six years. (She received her fifth nomination for *Silkwood* in 1984.) She had been nominated for best supporting actress in *The Deer Hunter* in 1978 and *Kramer vs. Kramer* in 1979, the year she won her first Oscar. In 1982, she was nominated in the best actress category for *The French Lieutenant's Woman*. With this win, she'd go down in history along with Maggie Smith, Helen Hayes, and Ingrid Bergman as the only actresses ever to hold Oscars for best actress and best supporting actress categories.

In Meryl's view, the statistics also pinpointed a big mistake. While she was filling her shelves with honors, she had been ignoring the theater. Mike Nichols, who'd also neglected his first love in favor of the screen, was ready to join Meryl in rectifying the error.

Ever since he lost the opportunity to direct her in

Private Lives, Nichols had wanted to bring Meryl to the stage. He'd been floored by her screen presence in his *Silkwood*; now was the time, he thought, to bring her back to Broadway. And he found an ideal vehicle: Tom Stoppard's comedy *The Real Thing*.

The witty, pun-filled play about an adulterous couple had been packing the house in London's West End with *Nicholas Nickleby* star Roger Rees its main attraction. Its art-mocks-life theme tickled Meryl's fancy, as did the numerous quotes from Strindberg's *Miss Julie*, the first drama Meryl ever did onstage as a freshman at Vassar.

But there were several drawbacks. Press agents for Stoppard said Meryl "balked at certain steamy scenes," and wanted the playwright to rewrite them. She may be able to get away with "creative contributions" in film, but theater was a different animal. Stoppard refused. Then his people said she didn't like the part because it wasn't a lead. The infighting continued. To sweeten the pot for Meryl, the producers signed Jeremy Irons, her partner in *The French Lieutenant's Woman*, to take over Rees's part. She reconsidered. Finally, she turned it down. Glenn Close, whose stage role Meryl had performed in the TV version of Wendy Wasserstein's *Uncommon Women and Others*, got the part instead.

23

VASSAR REDUX

Losing the part mattered little in light of her secret role.
Meryl was pregnant again.

And she'd been booked for a one-day performance that would take much preparation. Her role was the venerable pundit, the would-be inspiration to hundreds of young people. She had one long monologue, and, like her courtroom scene in *Kramer vs. Kramer*, she wrote it herself. The costume was simple: a cap and gown. After twice refusing Vassar College's offer to be the honored speaker at graduation, Meryl finally agreed to give the 119th commencement address.

When dawn broke on Vassar's graduation day, May 22, 1983, nobody could tell. Rain barreled down in the deep valley of Poughkeepsie and blackened the sky. Vassar president Virginia Smith awakened early and pictured a mud slide on the campus hill where degrees are traditionally conferred in view of thousands of onlookers. She immediately began to consider alternate graduation sites; high on her list was the recently completed gymnasium, a building that could seat only half of the expected guests. She thought of all the favorite aunts who'd have to be refused entrance for lack of space, the emeritus professors who returned every year to the campus for the ritual, and the housemothers who dressed up for the day to see the students pick up the diplomas. It was unlike President Smith, but she decided to postpone the site change. She'd give the weather another couple of hours to cooperate.

And the rains came even harder. The Taconic State Parkway, a narrow, winding road with as many turns as a corkscrew, was flooded in spots. Meryl heard the reports as she dressed Gippy. He and Gummer and Meryl's parents were also invited to attend the ceremony. On the drive up, the windshield wipers syncopated conversation. It was just as well. Meryl had a bad case of laryngitis. She sat quietly and held on to her speech while Gippy dozed. The only good thing was that the academic robes would mask her pregnancy.

President Smith decided to risk the outdoor ceremony when she saw that scores of reporters and a couple of TV crews had arrived. They came to Vassar only for Meryl, but to refuse them entrance might encourage a scene. And their annoying presence wouldn't be so noticeable outdoors. Unless, of course, the rain ruined their purpose. If it rained, everybody would be miserable.

As a joke, Meryl put on a pair of sunglasses as she followed in the procession of students marching past her special Vassar spots: Main Building, where she had lived during her senior year; Shakespeare Garden, a square patch blooming with heather, thyme, and all the other plants Shakespeare mentioned in his plays; the library; the president's house; the chapel. As she got to the top of the muddy hill and waited for the students to file into their folding chairs, the clouds began to lift. By the time she arrived at the foot of the outdoor theater, the sun was bright. "This lady is magic," said one student. "What did you expect from a WASP who speaks Polish?" asked his friend. It was a triumphant return to the place Meryl says "changed her life."

Gippy fidgeted in the front row, flanked by her husband and parents. Why couldn't he be good, Meryl thought. She often raved about him as "a centered child, not a race-around-and-tear-'em-up kind of kid." When he first visited her parents, they were astounded. "They were prepared to remove all the bibelots," Meryl says. "But Henry usually studies things. He picks up an object, examines it, and then carefully puts it down." Not today. He looked ready to run wild. On her way to the podium, Meryl gave Gippy a stern look.

She thanked President Smith and the members of the board of trustees for inviting her. "However, with your indulgence," she said to the grown-ups in black robes and colorful hoods designating their academic disciplines, "it is the class of 1983 to whom I wish to address my remarks and my heartiest congratulations this morning.

"I graduated from Vassar in 1971, that's twelve long years or twenty minutes ago, depending on how you look at it. Most of you were nine or ten; a few, precocious eight-year-olds. It's perhaps my presumption, then, that I do regard you as peers. I'd like to talk to you this morning as friends, and share with you a little of what I know about this transition you're about to make."

Then she dropped her speech. "I'm good at this," she told the 550 graduating seniors and their families. She had done the same thing a month earlier at the Academy Awards.

"Vassar is, and it was for me, the halcyon days. Real life is actually a lot more like high school. The common denominator prevails. Excellence is not always recognized or rewarded. What we watch on our screens, whom we elect, are determined to a large extent by public polls. Looks count. A lot. And unlike the best of the college experience, when ideas and solutions seem attainable if you just get up early, stay up late, try hard enough, and find the right source or method, things on the outside seem vast and impossible, and settling, resigning oneself, or hiding and hunkering down becomes the best way of getting along.

"Why did you ask me here to speak?" she questioned the students. "What do you think I know? Or, what do I represent that you want to know about?" A low-flying plane circled overhead. "See?" she said in an aside. "It's not always fun. They're always following me."

She continued her speech. "When I asked myself why you invited me here, I said, 'Okay, you represent success to them. You went to Vassar, got out, and did what you wanted to do and are richly rewarded for it. Two Oscars, two kids, almost. They asked you here to speak because they imagine you know why this happened to you. They imagine it could happen to them, too, and please could you please tell them how to set things up so that it does. Also, some of you would like to know how tall Dustin Hoffman is, and what does it feel like to kiss Robert De Niro?'

"You'll never know." She grinned wickedly.

"What I would like to tell you about today is the unsuccessful part, unsuccessful in that I'm not finished yet. That is the part of 'real life' for which Vassar did begin to prepare me: the investigation of my motives along the way, the process of making choices, and the struggle to maintain my integrity, such as it is, in a business that asks me to please just strip it off sometimes.

"What you can take away from Vassar is a taste for excellence that needn't diminish. Sometimes, I've wished it would go away, because some so-called important scripts are *so* illiterate, and the money is *so* good, that I've been tempted to toss all my acquired good taste, and hustle.

"But there's always the knowledge, and this *is* from experience, that the work itself is the reward, and if I choose challenging work it'll pay me back with interest. At least, I'll be interested, even if nobody else is.

"That choice, between the devil and the dream, comes up every day in different little disguises. I'm sure it comes up in every field of endeavor and every life. My advice is to look the dilemma in the face and decide what you can live with. If you can live with the devil, Vassar hasn't sunk her teeth into your leg the way she did mine.

"But that conscience, that consciousness of quality, and the need to demand it can galvanize your energies, not just in your work, but in a rigorous exercise of mind and heart in every aspect of your life. I firmly believe this engagement in the attempt for excellence is what sustains the most well-lived and satisfying, successful lives.

"What I'm telling you is that it goes so fast, and gets complicated so quickly, that remembering who you are and how you got there and what you really, really care about takes a hard, and frequent, shake-up effort. Add to this the hyperbolic life of celebrity, the intrusion of extreme self-consciousness onto every pubic utterance, and you have the reason I turned down this opportunity to speak several times in the past few years. You have the reason that many people who make it big very often hide out and hunker down; take care of business; don't extend themselves beyond the pressing demands of a major career, which will devour any amount of time you want to give it.

"But I've found as my networks expand and my responsibilities multiply, so does my future stake in the world, and instead of feeling the desire to keep quiet I feel the need to demand the best of our leaders, to secure the quality of the life my children will live in the next century, to secure the *fact* of their survival into the next century. In other words, to take it seriously, I must obey this incentive to excellence—not just in making a scene work, but in making 'the scene,' in participating fully and taking responsibilities we all share as citizens of the earth.

"We are all political actors, aren't we, to be judged by our sins of omission as well as commission, by our silences as much as our expressed opinions, by what we let slide as much as by the things we stand for?

"I've tried to count the number of interviews I've done lately with very well-meaning, well-educated journalists whose purported interest was in getting to the 'real me,' my most private concerns, my innermost thoughts. Recently, I traveled to Europe to publicize *Sophie's Choice*, and met more than thirty-five journalists there in four weeks. This process is sometimes fun, and sometimes really boring. The questions are basically the same on both sides of the Atlantic, with one startling difference. In Europe, as a matter of course, along with, 'How do you manage to combine family and career?' and 'How do you pick your scripts?' and 'What is your real hair color?' there would inevitably be a category of questions on the state of the world. It was just assumed, without any embarrassment at all, that as a member of the human race I had one or two thoughts on the subject. This from Swedes and Spaniards, Italians, Germans, English, and French. Everybody. Everybody but the home team. Now why is that? The American journalists never ask that.

"I think we feel in this country that it's 'inappropriate' for even the most vaguely expressed political views to intrude on what should be short, sparkling, and entertaining. Anyhow, I'm not going to try to make you share my political views today, but I do exhort you to investigate your own and follow through on them.

"Integrate what you believe into every single area of your life. Take your heart to work, and ask the most and best of everybody else, too. Don't let your special character and values, the secret that you know and no one else does, the truth—don't let that get swallowed up by the great chewing complacency.

"Good luck. And welcome to 'the big time.'"

Meryl stood at the foot of the grassy knoll, in the center of a bower of trees bordering a lake. The finale of her compelling speech brought tears and cheers from the students and their parents. "When she runs for office," said one gowned graduate, "that's when I'll begin to vote."

For the time being, Meryl is too busy for a political career. She delivered a healthy seven-pound, one-and-a-half-ounce baby girl on August 4, 1983. Meryl named her Mary Willa. "She is," says Meryl, "almost too good to be true."

Like mother, like daughter.

24

THE FUTURE IS THE PAST

During a re-evaluation of her career in 1984, Meryl began to search for acting projects that would re-unite her with old friends and fellow artists. It was as if she wanted to re-live the excitement of her early days with the people who first encouraged her in stage and screen work.

As she intimated in her commencement address to the Vassar graduates, Meryl must not have disliked Robert De Niro's screen kisses in *The Deer Hunter*. Soon after that speech, she signed a contract with Paramount Pictures to co-star with De Niro in *Falling in Love*, directed by Ulu Grosbard, and touted in preproduction as "the *Kramer vs. Kramer* of 1984."

In the screenplay by Pulitzer Prize–winning Michael Cristofer, Meryl plays Molly Gilmore, a doctor's childless wife from Scarsdale.

On the Metro-North commuter train, she meets De Niro, who plays Ben Cooper, a married architect from Hartsdale. He's on his way to work in Midtown. She's diligent about visiting her ailing father on the Upper East Side.

They get together after several more rides on the commuter train.

"It's an old-fashioned love story," said one Paramount executive.

It's also a New York City story. Apart from the two Westchester sites and a Brooklyn-brownstone rendezvous, all the movie's action takes place in Manhattan.

Such location shooting pleases Meryl. Although she has accepted the role of Isak Dinesen in Sydney Pollack's version of *Out of Africa*, which will take her to Kenya, she prefers to be near her family. For the same reason, Mike Nichols's proposal that they work together on the movie version of Nora Ephron's best-selling novel *Heartburn*, also excites her. It is set on the Upper West Side—and, as it happens, in the winter of 1984 the Gummers bought a nine-room co-op apartment on Central Park West.

That same winter, thanks to Meryl's fundraising efforts, a theater company close to her heart was given a permanent home just blocks from her new apartment. She raised thousands of dollars and agreed to participate in a musical comedy benefit for the Second Stage, a company dedicated to giving contemporary plays a second chance at production.

The Second Stage had been the testing ground for John Cazale. Meryl's continued involvement with the company might be viewed as an homage to her first love.

When the theater opened in mid-winter in a converted gymnasium on Broadway and Seventy-sixth Street, Second Stage director Carole Rothman named it the Walter McGinn/John Cazale Theater. Miss Rothman is the widow of McGinn, an actor who died in a car accident in 1977. Cazale, who was McGinn's best friend, died only one year later.

Let the circle, Meryl seems to say, be unbroken. In the spring of 1984, she and Joseph Papp, the New York Shakespeare Festival producer who first recognized her talents, announced plans to bring David Hare's award-winning drama, *Plenty*, to the screen.

The play's heroine, like Meryl herself, is intelligent, popular, complex, attractive, rich, and principled. But these assets ultimately lead to her downfall. Ineluctably, the "plenty" of the title becomes "too much." For all Meryl's own good fortune, she too worries that success corrupts idealism. It's the biggest issue in the career of this reluctant superstar.

INDEX

INDEX